The Mysticism of Everyday

Edward Carter, S.J.

Sheed & Ward

Sheed & Ward™ is a service of National Catholic Reporter Publishing Company, Inc.

Library of Congress Catalog Card Number: 90-63487

ISBN: 1-55612-410-4

Published by: Sheed & Ward
            115 E. Armour Blvd. P.O. Box 419492
            Kansas City, MO 64141

To order, call: (800) 333-7373

Contents

Acknowledgments

Scripture selections are taken from the *New American Bible With Revised New Testament*, Copyright© 1986, Confraternity of Christian Doctrine, Washington, D.C., and are used with permission. All rights reserved.

From *Foundations of Christian Faith* by Karl Rahner English translation© 1978, Crossroad Publishing Company. Reprinted by permission of The Crossroad Publishing Company.

Preface

In recent years we have witnessed an increased interest in mysticism. One manifestation of this has been the considerable attention which numerous people have given to non-Christian eastern religions with their mystical elements. Perhaps some of those who have directed their eyes eastward have been Christians who have erroneously thought that their own Christian religion had but little to offer them regarding the mystical element of religious experience. This misconception is far from the truth.

The Christian tradition is rich in mysticism, and in recent times we have witnessed a resurgent interest in the topic. Attention being given to books and lectures on myticism is quite significant. This marks a considerable change from the recent past. One has to go back only several decades to realize that at that time interest in mysticism was at a very low level.

Much of the traditional literature and teaching on Christian mysticism has been centered on the phenomenon of infused contemplation. We may also refer to this as classical mysticism. Classical mysticism, in turn, focuses considerable attention on that most special experience of God which the classical mystic enjoys.

A fascinating element of the current renewal of interest in Christian mysticism, however, is the attention being directed towards a more ordinary form of mysticism. This type has various names: hidden or latent mysticism, the mysticism of eveyday life, ordinary mysticism. Karl Rahner and Harvey Egan have been two contemporary theologians who have promoted this concept of the mysticism of everyday life.

In this particular book, I have chosen to focus attention on this more ordinary form of mysticism. While not completely omitting discussion of classical mysticism, I have concentrated attention on that type of mysticism which, seemingly, a considerable number of people experience. Some of these people are apparently unaware of their own mystical experience, shrouded as it is in its non-classical mode.

The current interest in the mysticism of everyday could well be a strong current in the future development of mystical thought, for the concept of ordinary mysticism has the advantage of relating to the experience of many more people than does that of classical mysticism. Also, the concept of ordinary mysticism makes it considerably easier to equate the highest development of the Christian life with the mystical state. Finally, the concept of the mysticism of everyday readily reminds us that the mystical life consists in a process, a way of life; it is much more than the occasional occurence of peak mystical experiences. Indeed, the idea of the mysticism of everyday life can teach us much about the spiritual life.

Edward Carter, S.J.
Xavier University
Cincinnati

Chapter One

The Basic Nature of Christian Mysticism

Mysticism has captured the attention of many present-day religionists. Writings on the topic have proliferated very noticeably. This contemporary interest certainly manifests a desire to experience more deeply the life of the spirit. Some, no doubt, have been thrust in this direction because they have undergone the disappointment which is the necessary consequence of pursuing the empty promises of materialism. Others, who have basically been following the God-appointed path of proper human living, feel an inexorable call to experience more deeply the God who invites them to higher things.

If many, therefore, are exhibiting a keen interest in the subject of mysticism, not all view it in an univocal way. The various views on mysticism cover a wide spectrum. Besides the Christian view, there are numerous other mystical traditions. The non-Christian East has long manifested a significant interest in the mystical aspect of human life. Buddhism, Hinduism, and Islam, among others, would certainly be discussed in any treatment of mysticism and world religions. Besides the more traditional views, other concepts of mysticism, including the very bizarre, have also assumed a position along the spectrum of mystical thought.

The psychologist and philosopher William James lists four characteristics of mysticism. While these are not completely adequate to explain the essentials of all mystical systems, they do offer considerable insight. James says the mystical experience is *ineffable*—one cannot adequately describe it. The experience is also *noetic*—it possesses a special type of knowledge. James also says mystical experience is a *transient* one—it is sustained for only relatively short periods. Finally, he says mystical experience includes a definite feeling of *passivity*—the distinct sensation of being possessed by a higher power.[1] Where we ourselves differ from James' view will become apparent as we progress.

While recognizing the existence of non-Christian mystical traditions, our own purpose is to discuss Christian mysticism. As we begin, we will find it helpful briefly to consider the basic meaning of the word mysticism.

The terms mysticism and mystic are related to the word mystery. The term mystery suggests that which is hidden and secret. Its use in a religious sense predates the event of Christianity. For example, its usage is associated with Hellenistic religious rites and with the secret doctrines of Egyptian hermeticism.[2] In turn, the word mystic refers to one who has been initiated into the hiddenness of the mystery.

In applying the concept of mysticism to Christianity, let us begin by listening to the words of St. Paul: "When you read this you can understand my insight into the mystery of Christ, which was not made known to human beings in other generations as it has now been revealed to his holy apostles and prophets by the Spirit, that the Gentiles are coheirs, members of the same body, and copartners in the promise in Christ Jesus through the gospel" (Ep 3:4-6).

God, the ultimate mystery, the ultimate hidden one, reveals himself and his plan for us in Christ Jesus. Through the gift of baptism we are initiated into this mystery of Christ. Through Christian faith we achieve a knowledge of God and the things of God unknown to those without this faith. The hiddenness of God becomes, in certain ways, revealed to us. True, God always remains mystery, for even with faith we do not fully comprehend him. Even though our intellects are elevated through faith, we still possess only a finite knowing—we cannot, therefore, perfectly comprehend the infinite God.

Through our incorporation into Christ, however, we do learn much about God and the plan which in his marvelous love he has designed for us in Jesus. Through our incorporation into Christ we do truly become mystics—persons who have received initiation into the mystery. We are all, then, in the very basic sense of the word, mystics. Thils states the matter in this fashion, "Every Christian will understand . . . that this participation in divine life is, of its very nature, the mystical life in germ. . . . What other foundation for mysticism could we desire? What other source of mysticism could we expect? And, on the other hand, how could a Christian say he is in the state of grace and deny that he is by this very fact on the way to the Christian mystical life? Certainly, there is mysticism and mysticism. But the essential will always and incontestably be the participation in the life of God."[3]

Although in a general sense, then, we are all mystics by our very baptism, the words mysticism and mystic are for the most part used only in regard to those who have developed the God-life to a very advanced degree. Let us take a more detailed look at this life.

Father, Son, and Holy Spirit have communicated themselves to us in a most intimate fashion. The intimacy and profoundity of this gift produce within us the image of the Trinity. Because Christ in his humanity mediates this Trinitarian gift, this image also possesses a Christic aspect. We receive this Christic, Trinitarian image in baptism. This image is our life of grace, our God-life, our Christ-life. St. Paul tells us, "Or are you unaware that we who were baptized into Christ Jesus were baptized into his death? We were indeed buried with him through baptism into death, so that, just as Christ was raised from the dead by the glory of the Father, we too might live in newness of life" (Rom 6: 3-4).

Through Christ, consequently, we share in God's own life—not in a pantheistic way, but, still, in a very real way. We are not God, but through the reality of grace we are God-like. Whether we use the terms Christ-life, God-life, the life of grace, Christic image, or similar phrases, we are speaking of this one reality. Growth in the mystical life, in turn, is characterized by an increasingly lived awareness that we do indeed participate in the life of God.

As St. Paul indicates in the above passage, this God-life possesses a Christic pattern. We have no other way to grow in God other than according to the teaching and example of Jesus. Indeed, Jesus himself has told us that he is the way, the truth, and the life.

Since Jesus' human existence is summarized in his paschal mystery—his death and resurrection—so also is our Christian existence. As Paul tells us above, we have been baptized into Christ, into his death and resurrection. This basic Christic pattern permeates Christian existence. As we variously assimilate the teaching and example of Jesus, as we relive his various mysteries, death-resurrection colors all. Yes, we continually die with Jesus so that we may increasingly rise with him. Assisted by the tender and loving care of Mary our spiritual mother—who is so closely associated with the work of her Son—and, guided by the Holy Spirit, we thus come closer to the Father in, with, and through Christ.

Karl Rahner succinctly reminds us how we are associated with Christ and his mysteries: "We can only get a complete picture of Christian existence, such as it is given by God and such as we should make it, if we take a good look at the whole life of Christ." And a little further on, Rahner tells us that Jesus still possesses the mysteries, the events, of his past existence: "Jesus has not lost a thing. He has not only saved His physical being intact, but everything has remained present, as it were, in its hidden, sublime essence." Finally, Rahner reminds us that in our union with Christ, we draw life from him as we relive his mysteries: "In other words, just as His cross and the totality of His life have become part of our life, so also is His Resurrection a factor in our present existence."[4]

This Christ-life we possess touches everything which is authentic in our lives. St Paul tells us, "So whether you eat or drink, or whatever you do, do everything for the glory of

God" (1 Cor 10:31). All that we do according to God's will in Christ, then, is an expression of the God-life, the Christ-life. Loving and being loved, tasting the sweetness of success as well as the bitterness of failure, feeling the joy of being accepted by others but also the pain of rejection—these human experiences give expression to the life of Christ within us. Enjoying the beauties of God's creation—he gorgeous sunset, the white-capped mountains spiraling skyward, the sun glistening through fall's brilliantly colored leaves—all this is living the Christ-life. Husband and wife experiencing both the joy and the pain of marriage and family life—through this also is God glorified. Experiencing the pain caused by the realization of the various and numerous social ills, but also knowing the satisfaction derived from our efforts to try to make this a better world—in this, too, we reflect Christ.

Living the various aspects of the human condition in Christ, then, is expressing Christian existence. Rahner states, "The basic and ultimate thrust of Christian life consists not so much in the fact that a Christian is a special instance of mankind in general, but rather in the fact that a Christian is simply man as he is. But he is a person who accepts without reservation the whole of concrete human life with all its advantages, its absurdities, and its incomprehensibilities."[5]

This Christic existence is centered in love. The Christ-life is a realization of how much God loves us. It is also a response to this love, a response which includes love of God, love of neighbor, love of self, love of all creation.

In striving to realize God's love for us, we should remember Jesus' teaching recorded by St. John. We should ponder these words, pray over them, assimilate them more and more, as we allow their meaning to penetrate to the innermost depths of our being: "For God so loved the world that he gave his only Son, so that everyone who believes in him might not perish but might have eternal life" (Jn 3:16).

This is our glory—God loves us. Strange, is it not, that we can allow this magnificent truth to fade to the background of our consciousness where it is not as life-giving as it should be. God loves each of us with a very deep and tender love. To realize this more and more is to realize the source of our life and growth. To grow in the conviction of this noble truth is to increase our sense of peace, a peace no one can destroy. To allow this realization to progressively dominate us is our key in handling properly the hardship and bitterness of life as well as its joy and happiness. To allow God's love to more fully possess us is to give ourselves over to a more committed response of love.

Our response to God's love for us includes love of God, love of neighbor, love of self. As Christian personalities we must harmoniously integrate these three dimensions. We should not think that the harmonious, integrated balance of these three dynamisms is achieved with little effort. Consistently to relate properly to God, others, and self is, rather, a sign of a mature Christian personality, a maturity which one usually achieves only over a considerable length of time.

Numerous examples demonstrate how individuals fail to balance properly these three aspects of Christian existence. For example, certain social activists have externally given themselves to the service of others in an inappropriate manner. They have, consequently, slighted their vertical relationship with God by neglecting prayer. Some, in striving for interiority through contact with more than the superficial self, go astray in various ways and develop a somewhat morbid introspection by failing to interact properly with others. There are also those who, because of the manner in which they concentrate on their vertical relationship with God, do not sufficiently realize and fulfill their responsibilities toward others. Consequently, they miss numerous opportunities for finding God in all things, for developing their horizontal relationship with God.

If, then, the harmonious blending of the thrusts toward God, neighbor, and self is not the easiest accomplishment, we should not think, on the other hand, that this balanced integration is almost impossible to achieve. If we truly commit ourselves to spiritual growth, this desired integration is, with God's grace, readily achievable. Furthermore, to experience the result of integrating these various aspects of Christian love is not an event we must postpone until we reach the highest degrees of spiritual maturity. On the contrary, we can, at any particular time, enjoy the intermingling of the various loves in a manner which is proportionate to the stage of our present spiritual development. Of course, the particular joy emanating from an advanced integration of love of God, neighbor, and self which is indigenous to the mature mystic personality will be of a higher nature than the joy beginners in the spiritual life experience. Again, the integration in question is an ongoing process, and it passes through many points on the path to a relatively full maturation.

The idea of spiritual maturation explicitly brings us back to the concept of mysticism, for mysticism—and here we are using the word to denote the mystical state—is the relatively full development of the Christian mystery within us. When a person develops the love-centered Christ-life to its state of maturity, that person is truly a mystic. We must properly understand the phrases, "relatively full development," "relatively full maturity." Such phrases indicate one has achieved a high degree of mature development, but that further growth is still possible.

The spiritual maturity which the mystic enjoys does not, in general, mean engaging in activities completely different than those experienced in less advanced stages of the spiritual life. The mystic still laughs and weeps, still rejoices in a task successfully completed, still feels the sting of failure, still enjoys a good meal and the camaraderie of friendly companionship. The spiritually mature mystic, however, now experiences all this on a deeper level, more at the center of his or her being. The mystic still sees, as it were, the same things, but sees the same things differently. The mystic now sees with a deepened faith vision, and acts with a deepened love dynamism.

We can view this stage of spiritual maturity—the mystical state—in terms of spiritual transformation. As William Johnston says, "Christian mysticism consists in living the

Christian mystery and being transformed by it."[6] The mystic has developed the Christic image to such an eminent degree that she or he lives the following thought of Paul on a higher plane than do those still traveling the lower regions of the spiritual life. Paul has left us these words, so dear to the heart of the mystic: "I have been crucified with Christ; yet I live, no longer I, but Christ lives in me; insofar as I now live in the flesh, I live by faith in the Son of God who has loved me and given himself up for me" (Gal 2: 19-20).

Notes

1. Cf. William James, *The Varieties of Religious Experience* (New York: Collier Macmillan, 1961), pp. 299-301.

2. Cf. Louis Bouyer, *Dictionary of Theology* (Tournai: Desclee Co., 1965), p. 313.

3. Gustave Thils, *Christian Holiness* (Tielt, Belgium: Lannoon, 1963), p. 557.

4. Karl Rahner, *Spiritual Exercises* (New York: Herder and Herder, 1965), pp. 244-47.

5. Karl Rahner, *Foundations of Christian Faith* (New York: Seabury Press, 1978), p. 402.

6. William Johnston, *Christian Mysticism Today* (San Francisco: Harper and Row, 1984), p. 185.

Chapter Two

The Mystical Process

We now wish to offer a brief, succinct outline of the mystical process. This entire work is, in various ways, a description of this process, but the advantage of having a preliminary sketch is obvious.

Since the mystical state is the culmination of the spiritual journey itself, it is clear that mysticism involves a continuing process. This is one point on which we disagree with William James. You will remember that in one of his characteristics of mysticism he describes the experience as being transient. No doubt he is speaking of those very special or peak experiences which occur along the mystical route.

In the Christian concept of mysticism, however, we should not think the mystical life is limited to these very special experiences. The Christian mystical life also includes many episodes of more diffuse, ordinary experiences. The mystical life is a process, a process which produces both an on-going purification and a deepening love union with God.

At this point it will be helpful to discuss the three basic levels of Christian mysticism. There is that very general level mentioned in the previous chapter. By our very incorporation into Christ, we have become partakers of the mystery, and thereby we are mystics. In the more elementary living of the Christ-life, then, we experience mysticism in a very general way.

As we previously indicated, however, the words mysticism and mystic are usually employed only regarding those who experience Christian existence in a superior fashion. We can explain what we mean in referring to this more advanced experience by listing the four characteristics of the mystical experience. Others, such as Poulain, list more than four. We think, however, these four include the essential notes of mysticism, all of which are intimately connected. What are these characteristics? Mysticism involves a more than ordinary experience of God; it has a noticeable element of passivity or receptivity regarding God's presence; it possesses a special loving wisdom or knowledge; it is a highly unifying experience regarding God, self, and neighbor.

Before we examine these four characteristics in some detail, we will conclude our statement referring to the three levels of mysticism. We said there is the very general level—the more elementary living of the Christian mystery. The second level, which brings us to the mystical life in the stricter sense, is the more than ordinary experience of God which includes the four characteristics—but only in a more sporadic fashion. The third level of mysticism is the mystical state itself in which one consistently experiences the four characteristics.

In giving a more detailed explanation of the characteristics, we begin with experiential aspects of mysticism. The mystical experience brings with it a realization of God and our participation in his life which is above the ordinary. Even though one experiences God only according to the framework of ordinary or latent mysticism, such an experience is still special and beyond that which the average Christian enjoys.

If the mystical life is experiential, it also includes the aspect of passivity or receptivity before God. To link the experiential dimension with that of passivity, we can state that the mystical experience of God is characterized by a noticeable receptivity. The mystic feels he or she is being especially guided by God, carried along by the divine impulse, possessed by God so that he or she may reflect himself or herself in a special way through this particular humanity. The mystic has a special awareness and conviction that she or he is living the God-life, the Christ-life. The experience of passivity or receptivity before God, however, does not mean a lack of effort and proper activity on the mystic's part. Indeed, the mystic puts forth more real activity than does the non-mystic. It is, however, an activity which is consequent upon the deep realization that God is the one who takes the loving initiative, and that our task is to be receptive to his voice. There are numerous examples of this disposition in the pages of Scripture. For instance, we read that Samuel was imbued with this attitude: "When Samuel went to sleep in his place, the LORD came and revealed his presence, calling out as before, 'Samuel, Samuel!' Samuel answered, 'Speak, for your servant is listening' " (1 Sm 3:9-10). We also read of Mary's perfect readiness to carry out God's design for her to be the mother of Jesus: "Behold, I am the handmaid of the Lord. May it be done to me according to your word" (Lk 1:38).

The third characteristic of mysticism is its loving wisdom or knowledge. The mystical experience produces a special knowledge concerning God and our participation in his life. For example, we all believe that God loves us. In the mystical experience, however, one grasps this truth with an experiential awareness which eludes the less advanced. Here we see the "hidden" aspect of mysticism come into play. We previously stated the connection of mysticism with mystery—mystery being that which is hidden or secret. The mystical experience yields a loving knowledge of God which is hidden—that is, one achieves it only by the especially close union with God which mysticism actuates. William Johnston observes, "The mystics of the Dionysian tradition speak frequently about the 'secrecy' of mysticism—mystical knowledge is 'hidden' in the depths of one's being."[1]

The fourth characteristic of mysticism is its profound unifying force. Mysticism produces a profound love union with God, neighbor, and the Christic self. The mystic is basically a lover. The mystic has a great and ever-increasing desire to hand over the self to God and to be more and more transformed into the divine—to become a particular expression of the infinite. Living the Christ-life to the fullest, the mystic offers Christ a new humanity through which he may manifest anew his life and mission. Being so closely united in love with God through Christ, the mystic simultaneously also achieves a deep love-union with the neighbor and the self. To love God is also to love his image in others and ourselves. To reiterate, the mystical process is a process of love.

Mysticism's four characteristics will variously manifest themselves throughout the mystical process. In the lower stages of the mystical journey they will appear only sporadically. Their appearance, however, leaves a deep impression upon a person.

For example, from time to time a person will become especially aware of God's love. This experience, although brief, leaves one with a significant source of strength. This mystical act of experiencing God's love in a more than ordinary fashion carries with it the four characteristics. First, it is a more than ordinary experience of God. Secondly, it produces a distinct consciousness of being open to God, of being receptive to his action. One has a desire to be increasingly possessed and guided by his love. Thirdly, this mystical act also gives an experience of loving, mystical knowledge—a knowledge of God and his love which does not accompany the more ordinary Christian experience. Fourthly, this mystical act of being especially aware of divine love is highly unitive—it produces a special, loving union with God.

As one progresses along the mystical journey, the experience of mystical acts becomes increasingly frequent. These acts finally achieve that consistency which allows entry into the mystical state—that stage of spiritual development in which a person experiences the four characteristics in a consistent fashion. Even in the mystical state, however, the degree of intensity of mystical acts can vary.

Throughout the mystical process, one can experience the four characteristics in a variety of fashions. Sometimes the experience is filled with sweetness and consolation. At other times, there can be darkness, or aridity, or severe trials or temptations. There can also be episodes of tranquillity coupled with ongoing aridity. Indeed, there are numerous possibilities. At all times, one must strive to be at peace in the Lord. Sometimes this is accomplished with relative ease; at other times one must strive valiantly to maintain this spiritual peace.

The pattern of death-resurrection permeates the mystical process. It can be no other way, since this was the summary pattern of Jesus' own existence. The mystic consitently experiences dying and rising with Jesus. Mystical dying produces a continuing purgation—a gradual purification which increasingly puts to death that which is not according to Christ. This results in a greater love-union with God, self, and others.

There are various ways to experience and express this death-resurrection experience. That of John of the Cross is not the only way, but he has given a classic description in his writings: "It now remains to be said that, although this happy night brings darkness to the spirit, it does so only to give it light in everything; and that, although it humbles it and makes it miserable, it does so only to exalt it and to raise it up; and although it impoverishes it and empties it . . . it does so only that it may enable it to stretch forward, divinely, and thus to have fruition and experience of all things, both above and below . . . ."[2]

As one experiences the mystical process, there is a growing realization of God's love for us. There is an increasing awareness that God's love is always taking the initiative, and that the Christian's task is to be open to this love. This love de- sires to possess us more deeply, to guide us to a more mature conformity to the divine will. God in his love for us desires to deepen our Christic, Trinitarian image—to give us an increased participation in the divine life, thus enabling us more fully to enjoy the indwelling presence of Father, Son, and Holy Spirit.

Increased mystical growth possesses, then, an evolving consciousness that we are to live the God-life, the Christ-life. William Johnston, in the introduction to his edition of the mystical classic, *The Cloud Of Unknowing*, comments on this awareness of the God-life.   In speaking of the anonymous author of *The Cloud*, he observes, "At the beginning . . . he makes a statement that echoes throughout the whole work: 'He is your being and in him you are what you are.' Lest this sound pantheistic, the author quickly adds, 'He is your being, but you are not his,' as if to remind us that while God is our being we are not God.   But having made this distinction he keeps stressing that the great suffering and illusion of man is his failure to experience that God is his being. . . . It is not in isolation that man finds his true self, but only in God."[3]

The prophet Jeremiah offers a vivid example of this living by the life of God:

> The word of the LORD came to me thus:
> Before I formed you in the womb I
>   knew you,
> before you were born I dedicated
>   you,
>   a prophet to the nations I ap-
>   pointed you.
>
> "Ah, LORD God!" I said,
> "I know not how to speak; I am
>   too young."
>
> But the LORD answered me,
> Say not, "I am too young."
> To whomever I send you, you shall
>   go;
> whatever I command you, you
>   shall speak (Jer 1: 4-7).

It is interesting to note that the psychologist Carl Jung, who has attracted the attention of numerous contemporary Christians, also points out the necessity of living by the life of God if one is to achieve personality maturity.   Mary Wolff-Salin, a Jungian commentator, observes, "All proportion guarded, Jung's Archetype of the Self is the way in which one experiences God. He will stress again and again the importance of learning to surrender to a greater power than one's own in the living of a deeper life. . . . . "[4]

In learning to live increasingly by the life of God, the mystic achieves an increased awareness of how helpless one is without God. This awareness does not, however, cause anxiety and spiritual paralysis. Rather it yields increased spiritual vitality as one says with St. Paul, "Therefore, I am content with weaknesses, insults, hardships, persecutions, and constraints, for the sake of Christ; for when I am weak, then I am strong" (2 Cor 12:10).

As the mystic is thus simultaneously aware of her or his helplessness and is convinced of the necessity of increasingly living by the life of God—living the Christ-life—the person grows in the realization that trust in God is imperative. Increased abandonment into God's arms requires increased trust. The mystic Julian of Norwich reminds us that God does indeed want our trust. She tells us, ". . . he wishes to be sought, and he wishes to be expected, and he wishes to be trusted."[5]

Humility is also very much at the heart of the mystical process. Progress in humility accompanies growth in the realization of how helpless we are without God. One of the greatest mystical teachers, St. Teresa of Avila, stresses the need for humility, ". . . have humility and again humility."[6]

Humility is a realization of our creaturehood. It is a realization that everything we have is a gift of God. The closer one approaches God in the mystical journey, the more this realization penetrates to the inner core of one's being. This evolving realization nourishes in the mystic the desire to increasingly abandon oneself to God's love. Increased humility also gives the mystic greater insight into his or her gifts and weaknesses. Consequent to this insight is a growing desire to develop further one's gifts and to labor at the diminishment of one's weaknesses—all this in order that the mystic may more dynamically reflect Christ.

Despite the importance of humility, it is a virtue which seemingly does not receive its proper attention in our present-day setting. It is certainly refreshing, consequently, to hear a contemporary psychotherapist articulate the role of humility in a person's development. In a chapter which deals extensively with the function of humility in one's personal growth, Mary Wolff-Salin observes, "In other words, both traditions—that of spirituality and that of depth psychology—point to the same kind of deviation which manifests itself in the same kinds of ways. Inflation or pride must be healed by the purifying therapeutic process supplied by continuing on the spiritual journey."[7]

Growth in true spiritual freedom is also a chief characteristic of the mystical process. The mystic achieves increased awareness of the necessity to be always open—to be truly free—to accomplish the divine will under the Spirit's guidance. The mystic is willing to take whatever means are necessary to shed more and more the shackles of one's non-freedom which prevent a person from accomplishing God's will. By non-freedom we do not mean that one is not responsible for deviation from the divine will, but that this abuse of one's free choice is actually a type of enslavement and therefore can be called a type of non-freedom. The maturing freedom to seek God by relating to persons, occupations, places, and things according to his will—this is the only pursuit which really interests the mystic. To pursue anything else is to follow the path of falsehood, regression, illusion, and consequent unhappiness.

The mystical process we have been describing does not remove us more and more from the human condition. On the contrary, it inserts us more deeply into the same. The mystic's experiential awareness of life in Christ is entirely appropriate to whatever is at hand. The mystical experience does not make one less present to work and people. Rather the mystic approaches all activity with greater depth. The mystic possesses a depth of faith-vision and love-dynamism which the more ordinary Christian lacks. This faith-vision and love-dynamism reach out and touch whatever the mystic happens to be doing.

This greater depth the mystic brings to everyday life results from living the really real in a manner which is foreign to the less advanced. With deep faith the mystic is more or less consistently aware of God's way of seeing reality. The mystic has a firmly rooted vision of the only completely real order which exists—that established in Christ. The mystic responds to this vision with a deep love. This love can be very dry at times, but its real depth is there. The mystic loves God deeply, loves people deeply, loves all creation deeply. The uninformed Christian tends to think of a mystic as someone who is withdrawn, whose humanness is clouded over with eccentricity. The opposite is true. The mystic is one who lives the really real to a high degree. The mystic lives as anyone logically should desire to live. The mystic has the desire to live life to the fullest according to the designs of God. The mystic, permeated with this desire, has taken the necessary means to achieve this cherished goal.

Notes

1. William Johnston, *The Inner Eye of Love* (San Francisco: Harper and Row, 1982), p. 37.

2. St. John of the Cross, *The Dark Night*, translated by E. Allison Peers (New York: Doubleday, 1959), Bk. 2, Ch. 9, p. 119.

3. *The Cloud of Unknowing*, edited by William Johnston (New York: Doubleday, 1973), p. 13.

4. Mary Wolff-Salin, *No Other Light: Points of Convergence in Psychology and Spirituality* (New York: Crossroad, 1986), p. 18.

5. Julian of Norwich, *Showings*, translated by Edmund Colledge and James Walsh (New York: Paulist Press, 1978), p. 194.

6. St. Teresa of Avila, *Interior Castle*, translated by E. Allison Peers (New York: Doubleday, 1961), Fourth Mansions, Ch. II, p. 83.

7. Wolff-Salin, *op. cit.*, p. 33.

Chapter Three

Mysticism and Love

As we previously stated, the mystical process focuses on love. Mysticism entails an evolving realization of how much God loves us, a realization which prompts the mystic to deepen his or her response to this love. Here then, are the aspects of love which increasingly consume the mystic's attention—God's love for us, our love for God, our love for God's creation—including, of course, love of neighbor and love of self. Let us now elaborate upon certain of these aspects of love.

It sounds so obvious to say God loves us; however, to voice this fundamental truth is not the same as allowing it to influence our existence as it should. On the other hand, the more we allow this truth to penetrate into our inner core and more dynamically direct our thinking and acting, the more we allow the words, "God loves us," to become truly life-promoting, and not merely an intellectual assent to an obvious truth. With God's grace, then, we must keep striving for a deeper comprehension of God's love. This love has brought us into existence, has redeemed us, has given us a mission in life. As we give ourselves over to the mystical process, the realization of these truths grips us with an enthusiasm which formerly eluded us. If acted upon, this realization truly transforms us.

God is ever with us. In his desire to take deeper possession of us, he asks us to be more receptive to his presence. God loves us, and he is our supporting rock, the one who will never fail us, the only one who can be our complete fulfillment. We must be determined to allow God in his love for us to be our life, our strength, our source of growth, our happiness. We must say with St. Paul, "What will separate us from the love of Christ? Will anguish, or distress, or persecution, or famine, or nakedness, or peril, or the sword? . . . No, in all these things we conquer overwhelmingly through him who loved us. For I am convinced that neither death, nor life, nor angels, nor principalites, nor present things, nor future things, nor powers, nor height, nor depth, nor any other creature will be able to separate us from the love of God in Christ Jesus our Lord" (Rom 8: 35-39).

Why are we sometimes afraid of God's love? We can shy away from the white heat of this love, foolishly thinking God will ask too much of us. When has God ever asked anything of us without giving us the grace to accomplish this? When has our heavenly Father ever asked that which has not brought us closer to him and thereby increased our happiness?

The mystics have marvelled at this love of God for his children. Embraced by this love, their fear has diminished and their trust increased. Made secure in this love, they have possessed the courage to undertake the ordinary with uncommon devotion and the heroic with dominant determination. Consumed with this love, they have continually pushed forward to accomplish more for Christ and his kingdom. Transformed by this love, the mystics have said with the most penetrating realization, "I have been crucified with Christ; yet I live, no longer I, but Christ lives in me; insofar as I now live in the flesh, I live by faith in the Son of God who has loved me and given himself up for me" (Gal 2: 19-20).

Obviously, we can never fully fathom the depth of God's love for us. We can, however, grow in what will always be a finite comprehension of this awesome reality. Christ has shown us his heart as a constant reminder that we should strive for a greater realization of what it means to say God loves us. The heart of Christ is indeed the symbol of God's fathomless love for us, a love which requests our own response of love.

Some of the mystics have explicitly told us about the treasures found in the heart of Christ. St. Bonaventure, a doctor of the Church, is one of these. In his *The Tree Of Life* he tells us how the Church and her sacraments have come forth from the heart of Christ: "Then, in order that the Church might be formed out of the side of Christ sleeping on the cross . . . the divine plan permitted that one of the soldiers should pierce open his sacred side with a lance. While blood mixed with water flowed, the price of our salvation was poured forth, which gushing from the secret fountain of the heart gave power to the sacraments of the Church. . . ."[1]

Christ's heart, then, is a vivid symbol of God's salvific love for us, a love which calls for our own response of love. What does our response include? As Jesus himself has told us, it includes love of God, love of neighbor, love of self. Let us further consider these aspects of Christian love.

Our love for God includes our attachment to him in all his infinite perfections—his goodness, love, mercy, justice, and so forth. Our love for him also includes his will for us as manifested in many different ways. This can be the difficult part of loving God. It is very easy for us to say we love the all-good God, but when God's will shows us how we are to live, we do not always give a ready response in love.

As we strive to love God by fulfilling his will in our lives, Jesus is our example and our inspiration. Christ's life was supremely successful because he perfectly loved his Father's will. In like manner must the life of each of us be judged— this life which is our response of love. At times we tend to judge the value of our lives not by first looking to God's will, but rather by primarily considering whether our work is enjoying success, whether we are being loved and accepted by others, whether we are feeling particularly worthwhile. Let us make ourselves very clearly understood here. We are not saying that an existence which possesses the above qualities cannot be one deeply conformed in love to God's will, and, therefore, a highly successful and valuable life. This, however, is not always the case. Sometimes our lives could possess the above characteristics and yet be considerably lacking in conformity to God's will; and to the extent that God's will does not influence us, our lives lack real value despite all the appearances to the contrary.

We can, on the other hand, be tempted to think our lives are useless, or, even worse, a nuisance to ourselves and others because of what appears to be unsuccessful living. We may presently be feeling the weight of a continual sense of frustration, or we may be experiencing a painful period of being misunderstood by others or having our work go un- noticed, or a particular trial seems to keep nagging at us— and the list could go on and on. Even though the suffering may be cutting very deeply, and our lives seem to lack suc- cess and value, we must realize through reflective faith that our own existence in the distressing here and now is greatly worthwhile provided we are reaching out to embrace God's will with love—yes, even though our love at the time may seem so weak, and frustrated, and almost shattered.

One of the greatest mystical teachers, Teresa of Avila, reminds us of the central position this loving conformity to God's will holds in the mystical journey. It is, she says, the key issue for the beginner in the spiritual life as well as for the most advanced: "All that the beginner in prayer has to do—and you must not forget this, for it is very important— is to labour and to be resolute and prepare himself with all possible diligence to bring his will in conformity with the will of God. As I shall say later, you may be quite sure that this comprises the very greatest perfection which can be at- tained on the spiritual road."[2]   And, again, ". . . love con- sists . . . in the firmness of our determination to try to please God in everything."[3]

If we become aware of the varied manner in which God manifests his will, and if we act upon the realization that our love for God dictates that we assimilate his will, then the seeds of mysticism given at baptism come more and more into bloom. Our lives will continue to rest upon solid ground and not upon sand. We will be implementing the teaching of Jesus: "Not everyone who says to me, 'Lord, Lord,' will enter the kingdom of heaven, but only the one who does the will of my Father in heaven" (Mt 7: 21).

As we grow in loving conformity to God's will, we increasingly live by the mutual sharing of gifts between God and ourselves. This concept is extremely important for understanding the mystical life. Progress in the mystical life, then, is centered in the increasingly lived realization of this basic fact: as Father, Son, and Holy Spirit have in love given themselves to us, together with a created participation in their life (our life of grace), we too make a love gift of ourselves to them. As this process takes deeper hold of us, God increasingly possesses our persons with all their faculties, and more and more is reflected through our persons. We are indeed finite expressions of the infinite God.

St. John of the Cross tells us how this mutual exchange of gifts between God and the Christian reaches its culminating point in the spiritual marriage—mysticism's highest stage: "It now remains for the said Spiritual Marriage to be made between the soul aforementioned and the Son of God. This is without comparison far geater than the Spiritual Bethrothal because it is a total transformation in the Beloved, wherein on either side there is made surrender by total possession of the one to the other with a certain consummation of union of love . . . ."[4]

Although the spiritual marriage marks the highest exchange between God and the mystic, it is very important to realize that a lesser exchange occurs in the lower realms of the spiritual life. God in his love is always calling the spiritual pilgrim, inviting her or him to receive his greater self-communication, inviting the person to make a greater gift of self to Father, Son, and Holy Spirit.

We have briefly discussed God's love for us and ours for him. As we progress in our treatment of Christian love, we remind ourselves that much of God's will for us pertains to our relationship with our neighbor. Love of God and love of neighbor are, indeed, inseparably linked. St. John, in a well-known Scriptural passage, vividly reminds us of this: "If anyone says, 'I love God,' but hates his brother, he is a liar; for whoever does not love a brother whom he has seen cannot love God whom he has not seen" (1 Jn 4:20).

The mystical process involves a maturing realization of why John's statement is true. Growth in the mystical journey includes an increased awareness that one is made in God's image. Increased awareness of this regarding oneself gives a proportionate consciousness of one's neighbor as also being in the divine image. To love God, then, necessarily means to love one's neighbor whose existence possesses the divine imprint.

Although we must, then, necessarily love all, this does not mean we must like everyone. There is a difference. There are certain personalities which do not appeal to us— we do not like them. We must, however, love them. Furthermore, regarding the wrong actions of anyone, I can and must reject such actions, yet I can and must love the core person who is in God's image.

The contemporary Christian has a special responsibility and privilege as bearer of love for one's neighbor. A Christian of any age certainly has a duty of love towards the human race, but our present-day world has special need of people who deeply love their brothers and sisters within the human family. We live in critical times. Enormous problems confront the human race, and many of these occur because there is insufficient love in the hearts of many. As we sweep our gaze across the world and observe what happens when there is this failure of love, we are aware of the special danger this lack of love produces in contemporary times. We live in a nuclear age. We must counterbalance the awesome threat of holocaust with increased effort to love our fellow human beings. Responding to God's grace, you and I must decide what this means for each of us.

Some today doubtlessly think that to talk of mysticism is to distract us from attending to the overwhelming needs of contemporary society. This attitude is nothing new. There have always been those who have thought that mysticism hinders a practical love and social concern for one's neighbor. Such an attitude is far from the truth. Growth in the authentic mystical process—as opposed to false mysticism— means growth in union with God. Greater union with God, in turn, means a greater capacity to be and to do for one's sisters and brothers. The lives of the mystics are outstanding witnesses to this statement. What they have accomplished for others comprises a remarkable story of loving concern for one's neighbor. They achieved all this, moreover, precisely because of their mysticism. As Dom Cuthbert Butler succinctly observes, ". . . the mystics were what they were, not in spite of their mysticism, but because of it."[5] William James, in speaking of one of these mystics, St. Ignatius Loyola, says, "Saint Ignatius was a mystic, but his mysticism made him assuredly one of the most powerfully practical human engines that ever lived."[6]

We have briefly discussed God's love for us, our love for God, and our love for neighbor. Finally, let us discuss love for oneself. This is an extremely important concept, one that has not always received proper attention throughout the history of Christian spiritual writing and teaching. The situation, happily, is changing today. Indeed, we must love ourselves, since we are in the image of God. As we cooperate with God in developing our Christic, Trinitarian image, we grow in the capacity to see our worth and lovableness. What John of the Cross says concerning the worth and loveableness of one who has achieved the spiritual marriage is proportionately true of those still walking in the lower regions of the spiritual journey: "When, therefore, the soul feels itself very near to going forth to possess its kingdom completely and perfectly, in the abundance wherewith it sees itself enriched (for it knows itself to be pure and rich and full of virtues and prepared for this . . .)."[7]

We are loveable, then, because God has clothed us with his beauty. Proper self-love, consequently, is a virtue. In love for the self we rejoice at how we have thus far participated through grace in the greatness of God; in love for the self we also determine to develop further this divine image.

True self-love, therefore, is far removed from the narcissistic self-love, the selfish love of self, which is so prevalent in today's culture. Narcissistic love has no concern for God and others. Such love focuses one's attention solely on the selfish interests of a person. It is interested only in the so-called personal fulfillment and satisfaction of the narcissistic individual. Because this falsely conceived fulfillment is based on selfishness, however, real fulfillment for the narcissist is impossible. Narcissistic love of self is really hatred of self, since it is totally opposed to the true good of the individual—life according to God.

Authentic love of self, then, is the love of the true self, the self possessing the Christic, Trinitarian image. This self desires to live according to God's plan. Part of this plan is the same for all human beings—God has a basic will according to which all must live in order to achieve happiness here and hereafter. In addition, God also has a special plan for each individual, since he has created each a unique person.

Love of self, consequently, involves growth in achieving self-identity—achieving an ever greater self-knowledge, an ever greater awareness of who I am as this unique, Christic, individual, an ever greater awareness of what God wants me to do with my life. Love of self also involves acting according to this awareness.

Getting to know myself would seem to be a simple process. After all, do I not consistently live on a very intimate basis with myself? I can tell myself, therefore, that self-knowledge comes with little effort. In fact, it is not all that easy. There are indications that in certain respects I do not know myself nearly as well as I had thought. At times people tell me something about myself of which I was hardly aware, and the number of persons concurring in this observation excludes the probability that they all are in error regarding their assessment. There is also the possibility that I may really think I have the talent for a certain occupation whereas in reality I possess very little potential for it. On the other hand, the talents I actually possess for some other work or profession I may only slightly recognize or recognize not at all. The significant number of people who have actually mistakenly assessed themselves should make me realize that erroneous self-evaluation in some regards is not an unrealistic possibility. To be unaware of the various possibilites of incorrect self-evaluation is to hinder growth in self-knowledge.

We also hinder growth in self-knowledge if we over-identify with the various personalities we assume. In Jungian terminology, these are called various personas or masks we assume in coping with the demands of a necessarily varied existence amid the complex human condition. A Jungian commentator, James Welch, observes regarding the persona, "A persona is a mask, or a number of masks, through which the individual relates to the world around. Masks are means of adaptation to society and a protection for the psyche. A raw psyche, without the mediation of a persona would be a jarring experience for the individual as well as society. . . . I have different masks for different occasions, and, consequently, different views of myself will be highlighted."[8] As necessary as the different personas are in the life of an individual, equally necessary is the ability not to equate my total self-identity with the personas. For example, if a person over-identifies with his or her work persona, failure in that work can occasion devastating loss of self-esteem, a sense of worthlessness, and concomitant depression.

Achieving adequate self-knowledge can be both painful and joyful. Coming to the realization that I have this bad trait, or that weakness, can be disturbing, frustrating, or humiliating—especially when others point out these negative characteristics. Growth in self-knowledge, however, can also be encouraging and joy-producing as I realize I can do something about these negative aspects, as I achieve a deeper insight into certain positive qualities or become aware of others that I hardly knew existed. The quest for self-knowledge can, then, be exciting. As I obtain better knowledge of both my limititons and my capabilities, I see interesting possibilities for more advanced Christian living which I have not yet implemented.

Growth in self-identity does not take place in a vacuum—the vacuum of the isolated self. Rather, I achieve self-knowledge through the proper relationship with reality. Through the interaction of myself with various facets of created reality—persons, places, things, happenings—I can come to know much about my strengths and weaknesses, my talents and limitations, my personality and temperament. It is, however, especially through my relationship with God that I grow in achieving self-identity. God, the ultimate source of all knowledge, is, consequently, the ultimate source of self-knowledge. God continually wants to remind me of the fundamental fact concerning myself—that he overwhelmingly loves me and that I am uniquely precious to him. Upon this rock-bottom fact rests all other facets of self-knowledge. Regarding all aspects of knowing myself, God is most anxious to help me grasp these with greater clarity. My task is to allow him to do so. If I open myself to him in prayer, he will continue to reveal himself to me, and also he will reveal *myself* to me. The more I fathom the mystical depths of my being—the more I allow God to lead me to the center of my being—the more God will tell me about himself and myself, this self which is in his image. Deeper insights concerning himself and myself come to light—and here again we meet up with the hidden aspect of mysticism. The more, in turn, I know of myself under God's guidance, the more I can truly love myself.

The ongoing assimilation of the various dimensions of love which we have been discussing is not without its pain. Some have learned this lesson well, others have not. Indeed, the real tragedy concerning human suffering is not that there is so much of it, but that apparently so much of it is wasted.

There are two basic responses to suffering—one correct, one incorrect. Let us consider a simple example. Two persons have have been partially paralyzed because of an accident. One becomes embittered by his fate, and becomes an enclosed-type person, one who refuses to go out in love to God and others. The second person, despite the frustration and disappointment, resolves to strive to continue to grow as a person, and determines to utilize this physical tragedy as a means of becoming a person who loves more deeply.

To grow in love, then, includes the willingness to cope properly with suffering, whatever its kind. Progress in love includes knowing how to use suffering as a means of growth. The mystic has learned this lesson well.

In summarizing this chapter, we can say that our purpose here on earth is to realize in Christ how much God loves us and to respond by loving God, our neigbor, ourselves, and all creation. Christian life, with its highest development occurring in the mystical state, is that simple. Here we speak of simplicity in the sense of unity—a concept marvelously attractive to mystics. The unity of which we speak is that which emanates from the facets of Christian love. This unity is not that which excludes rich variety and numerous possibilites. The more we realize God's love and give our love in return, the more we realize love is an ongoing process that never exhausts all the marvelous and myriad possibilities of its implementation.

Growth in the mystical process, since it both increases our awareness of these splendid truths and allows us to more deeply live them, is, then, an adventurous journey.

Notes

1. *Bonaventure: The Soul's Journey into God, The Tree of Life, The Life of St. Francis,* translated by Ewert Cousins (New York: Paulist Press, 1978), pp. 154-55.

2. St. Teresa of Avila, *Interior Castle,* translated by E. Allison Peers (New York: Doubleday, 1961), Second Mansions, p. 51.

3. Ibid. "Fourth Mansions," p. 76.

4. St. John of the Cross, *Spiritual Canticle,* translated by E. Allison Peers (New York: Doubleday, 1961), Stanza XXII, p. 372.

5. Dom Cuthbert Butler, *Western Mysticism* (New York: Dutton, 1924), p. 314.

6. William James, *The Varieties of Religious Experience* (New York: MacMillan, 1961), p. 324.

7. St. John of the Cross, *Living Flame of Love*, translated by E. Allison Peers (New York: Doubleday, 1962), Stanza I, p. 174.

8. James Welch, *Spiritual Pilgrims: Carl Jung and Teresa of Avila* (Ramsey: Paulist Press, 1982), pp. 89-90.

Chapter Four

Mysticism and Prayer

The Basic Nature of Christian Prayer

The Christ-life is a participation in God's own life. Faith is the vision aspect of this life. Through Christian faith we become participants in the knowing activity of God on a supernatural level. Our Christian faith allows us to share God's vision of all reality. It is interesting to observe that St. John the Evangelist has the concept of light as one of the great themes of his writings. At the center of his light theme is Jesus, the light of the world, he who comes to share his light with us, he who comes to give us the Father's vision of reality.

Even the sincere Christian can at times live merely on the surface or periphery of reality. He or she fails to comprehend sufficiently the inner core of reality, its more meaningful depths. As Christians we possess a faith-vision which allows us to see all reality as God intends us to view it. Our task is, with God's help, to activate this faith-vision and make it as consciously operative as possible, relative to all dimensions of our activity.

Faith-vision has a special source of actuation in prayer. Prayer, consequently, is of special importance for the Christian to attain insight into reality. This faith-vision or insight is intended not for the intellect alone. We can learn here from the general concept of biblical faith. The biblical view of faith stresses that faith commitment is not merely an assent of the intellect to Christ's truth but is a commitment of the total person. The situation is similar in prayer, which very much involves faith. The light of prayer should permeate the Christian's entire being. The light of prayer is intended to fire the will, to stir up the heart. The light of prayer has the capacity to help gather all one's forces and to direct them anew toward God, toward others, toward oneself, toward all creation. The light of prayer, then, helps relate the Christian properly to all reality.

Prayer not only gives this marvelous light but also a corresponding strength—the love, the determination, to live out properly one's relationship to reality, to reality as it is in its true nature, in its inner core, in its very depths.

If prayer renews our relationship with all reality, it most specially deepens our relationship with the ultimate reality, God himself. Prayer is a special actuation of what the Christian life is all about—in and through Jesus God communicates himself and asks for our response. The concept of personal presence, consequently, is essential for the understanding of prayer. In prayer we become especially attentive to God's presence in us. During prayer we possess a heightened awareness of how God gives himself to us and of what our relationship to him should be.

In prayer we should be open to God. Prayer should be more of a listening on our part than a speaking. We speak, yes—in response to God's word. God wishes to fill us with himself, and during prayer his self-communication can be especially lavish, although subdued and quiet for the most part.

Because God is giving himself in love, our openness in prayer is one of love. Love, then, characterizes and permeates the personal presence of prayer. In this atmosphere of love we feel secure. We realize that we still have faults to work against. We know we must grow and become more mature in many ways. Despite all this, we know that God loves us, and overwhelmingly so, that God loves each of us so tenderly and so uniquely, loves us much more than we love ourselves, loves us with expectations as he invites us increasingly to realize our tremendous potential, as he invites us to become more what we are meant to be.

Embraced by God in prayer, we can, in response to his self-communication, speak to him about anything and everything. We know that the more we love a human person, and feel loved by that other, the more we feel able to communicate with that person. Should we not, then, feel a desire to communicate with God, this God who loves us much more than any human person can, and whom we love above all else? Should we not feel perfectly at ease in talking to him about anything which is troubling us? Should we not be eager to share with him our joys, our successes, our enthusiasm, our failures, our pain?

Our prayer is mediated by Christ—this is simply an application of the fundamental truth that Jesus in the mediator between the Father and us in all things. Our prayer, then, should be rooted in Christ. It is important to realize that, varied as the manner of our prayer may be, we always approach the Father in and with Jesus, under the guidance of the Holy Spirit.

We can implement the Christocentrism of prayer by prayerfully considering the mysteries of Christ's life, allowing their consideration to penetrate us, allowing these events to shape our lives more according to Christ's image. Also, our Christ-consciousness during a period of prayer may take the form of allowing a particular teaching of Jesus to take deeper hold of us. While obviously not comprising an exhaustive list, these are a few examples of how our prayer can be Christocentric—Christian prayer. Yes, in prayer as at all times the Father wishes to speak to us through his Son. Under the Spirit's guidance we open ourselves to the Father's Christ-centered, love-centered message, and respond with a love of our own: "In times past, God spoke in partial and various ways to our ancestors through the prophets; in these last days, he spoke to us through a son, whom he made heir of all things and through whom he created the universe . . . ." (Heb 1:1-2).

To say that the interpersonal presence of prayer—God present to us and we to him—is permeated with love is not to say that prayer is always easy or devoid of difficulties. The pattern of death-resurrection applies to prayer as it does to all other aspects of Christian existence. We must be willing to die with Christ—to encounter the difficult, the painful—in order to rise more with him. This increased share in Jesus' resurrection means increased union with God.

What are some of the difficulties experienced in the life of prayer? There is the effort required to attain the self-discipline which one must exercise in the practice of prayer. All aspects of one's person—intellect, will, imagination, memory, emotions, body, and so forth—must be properly controlled in order to facilitate the special and very direct contact with God which prayer should produce. Regarding the control of intellect, imagination, and memory, such discipline will usually not eliminate all distractions. Higher mystical prayer is devoid of these distractions because of God's special grasp of the faculties, but in lower stages of prayer the pain of trying to control distractions is usually a rather common occurrence. Basil Pennington says, "If you ask friends who have been faithful in prayer what has been their greatest challenge, if they don't answer 'dryness', they will most surely say, 'distractions'."[1]

The maturing of the virtues during the life of prayer presents another type of suffering. Sometimes the suffering connected with this maturation process can become quite intense, as the writings of some of the saints indicate. God, however, is there, proportioning the suffering according to one's capacity, and giving the grace which enables one to sustain the trial. Experiencing God as very distant in prayer is an example demonstrating how the virtues are strengthened. One can even feel a sense of abandonment, although God is in reality very close. Hope is thus tested and fortified. Humility is deepened as one realizes his or her helplessness. Love grows as the person realizes one must seek God even though his gifts of consolation are for the present absent. In like manner do the other virtues also take deeper root.

It is opportune at this point to say a few words about the various methods of prayer. The essence of prayer is God present to us and we to him through our exercise of faith, hope, and love. Methods, then, are obviously a means to an end, not ends in themselves. Whatever method here and now seems best to place one in contact with God is the best method for that particular person at this point in her or his spiritual development. To put it in other words, we should pray according to the method which seems the most effective in establishing the prayerful awareness of God's presence, of his loving self-communication. Another good sign that our present method of prayer is the appropriate one is its productiveness of good in our daily lives. If prayer is sustaining us in our desire to follow Christ, if it makes us more eager to fulfill his will, if it aids us in loving him and our neighbor more, then we have assurance that our present method of prayer is the correct one.

Whatever method of prayer we use, the prayer itself, as it progresses, usually becomes less discursive and more simplified or contemplative. Again, we are stating what usually occurs. A person's prayer could progress while remaining considerably discursive, that is, characterized by relatively numerous and varied concepts and images. If there is true progress in such an instance, however, it would mean that the discursiveness was an effective means for this particular person in achieving a deeper contact with God through a more mature faith, hope, and love.

Contemplative Prayer

Simplified or contemplative prayer consists in a simple, loving gaze at God. The simplification involved in contemplative prayer is threefold. First, there is a simplification of the intellectual aspect of prayer. One thought tends to dominate. Other thoughts may be present, but they tend to come and go and do not possess any significant prominence. The dominant thought of contemplative prayer may simply be that of God's presence. Secondly, the acts of the will undergo the same basic simplification, and increasingly the various will-acts center in that of love. The third aspect of simplification extends to the entire spiritual life. This is one of the great advantages of simplified or contemplative prayer. The same predominant acts of intellect and will present in prayer overflow into one's entire life, bringing everything together in a unified harmony.

As prayer progresses into contemplative prayer, it becomes more passive or receptive before God's presence. We must understand, however, that this increased passivity or receptivity does not mean less activity on our part, but actually activity of greater intensity. One's activity now operates on a higher level. John Wright states the matter well:

> It is frequently said that the prayer of beginners is more active and that as time goes on and prayer matures it becomes more passive. . . . This means, of course, that our attitude becomes more passive. But our actual activity or operation doesn't in itself become less. There is indeed a greater dependence on God's action, and what we do is done more freely, more simply, more intensely and spontaneously. Our attention, then, is more upon God than upon ourselves, but we are actually more active in the real sense.[2]

What Wright says here concerning passivity in prayer, is proportionately true of the mystical life in general. The more the mystic progresses, the more he or she becomes passive or receptive before God. Yet this increased passivity leads to an increased activity on the mystic's part, one which is more mature, intense, and dynamic.

Besides possessing greater simplicity and passivity, contemplative prayer also possesses greater depth. In contemplative prayer a person descends more deeply toward the center of one's being, where God and the true or Christic self are simultaneously met on a more meaningful level. A modern movement, centering prayer, reminds us of the value of the type of prayer which becomes more vertical. Although not all would equate centering prayer with contemplative prayer—some apparently place it a step before it—at the very least there are significant similarities between the two. Centering prayer, for instance, has, as does contemplative prayer, a thrust towards greater depth and unification. As Basil Pennington observes, "There is no copyright on the name, 'Centering Prayer' . . . it is still being used in a general sense to refer to any method by which the pray-er seeks to bring his or her scattered thoughts and feelings together to allow for a certain deepening."[3]

Contemplative prayer, then, possesses these characteristics: it has a definite mark of simplication and unification; it produces in one's prayer life a very significant deepening; it possesses an increased passivity or receptivity before God.

How does one know if she or he is being called to contemplative prayer? First, one has difficulty in continuing to use the more discursive form of prayer. Also, one now has a certain distaste for this method of prayer, and the benefits which this type of prayer once yielded now seem considerably diminished. Secondly, one has a very distinct desire to be with God and to gaze upon him with a simple, loving look. Other signs will also accompany the initiation into what is called infused contemplation strictly so called, but for our purposes the above listing will suffice.

Contemplative prayer exists on three levels. There is the non-mystical level. On this level there may be sporadic experience of mystical acts. The four characteristics of mysticism are not, however, present in a consistent fashion. Contemplative prayer is also usually found in one who experiences what we may call ordinary mysticism. Lastly, contemplative prayer is experienced in a very special manner by the person who enjoys what we may call classical contemplation, a synonym for the more traditional term, infused contemplation.

Let us briefly look at each of these three forms of contemplation. Before we do so, however, it will be helpful to repeat the four characteristics of the mystical experience. The mystical experience yields a more than ordinary experience of God; it possesses a special type of loving wisdom or knowledge; it is very noticeably passive or receptive before God's presence, giving a heightened sense of dependence upon him; it produces a very intimate union with God.

In the practice of contemplative prayer on its lowest level, there will be the simple, loving gaze at God with the accompanying deepening of prayer and the increased passivity with its keen awareness of dependence upon God. This increased passivity or receptivity, however, is not consistent enough to situate the person in mystical prayer. The other three characteristics of mysticism are also experienced only in a more sporadic fashion. If, then, mystical acts are occasionally present on this lower level of contemplation, their infrequency still leaves a person basically on the non-mystical level of contemplation. Contemplation even at this stage, however, has numerous benefits as indicated above.

When a person's contemplative prayer consistently manifests the four characteristics of the mystical experience, such a person is practicing mystical prayer in the strict sense. This mystical prayer may be of the more ordinary or latent type, or of the classical type—infused contemplation.

The more ordinary kind of mystical contemplation produces a very distinct receptivity or passivity before God—passivity in the sense described in the above quotation from Wright. The person has a very definite sense of being possessed by God, of living by his life, of being completely dependent upon him. This awareness carries beyond the boundaries of formal prayer, and influences the person's attitude throughout the day. To become more and more a finite, human expression of the infinite God is the consummate desire of the contemplative. Whatever the task or activity at hand, the all-important aspect for the person is the accomplishment of God's will at the moment. Surrendering to the divine, the mystic allows God to be imaged in the here and now through this particular human person. Experiencing God and finitely expressing him is much more at the center of consciousness than in earlier stages of the spiritual life. Particular activities, of course, are still important—their importance is actually heightened in the person's awareness—but one increasingly sees these activities as being important precisely because one is experiencing God and reflecting God through them.

The heightened receptivity of the mystical contemplative is accompanied by the other three characteristics of mysticism—the greater receptivity or dependence on God includes a experience of God above the ordinary with its special kind of loving knowledge and an intimate union with God.

If the contemplative experiencing ordinary mysticism is conscious of God in a manner superior to the non-mystic, the person blessed with classical mysticism experiences God in a most special fashion. St. Teresa of Avila gives a description of this experience: "When picturing Christ in a way I have mentioned, and sometimes even when reading, I used unexpectedly to experience a consciousness of the presence of God, of such a kind that I could not possibly doubt that He was within me or that I was wholly engulfed in Him."[4] And, again: "God implants Himself in the interior of that soul in such a way that, when it returns to itself, it cannot possibly doubt that God has been in it and it has been in God . . . ."[5]

This very special sense of God's presence is called classical infused contemplation, or simply, infused contemplation. The qualifying word classical is useful, however, because all contemplation—indeed, all Christian prayer—has an infused element. This infused element is God's gift of grace. We will, henceforth, use the phrases infused contemplation and classical contemplation synonymously.

What explains the special sense of God's presence in classical contemplation? Theologians offer various explanations. The best explanation seems to be that of grace-become-conscious. Outside of infused contemplation we know by faith that God has given us a life of grace. Through the very special grace of infused contemplation a person experiences this truth in an extraordinary fashion. Faith becomes operative in a most special manner. In a sense we can say that she or he "feels" the life of grace. Through this medium of grace-become-conscious, the person has an extraordinary sense of God's presence.

In discussing the degrees of infused contemplation, theologians differ somewhat. We follow the classification of Joseph de Guibert who holds that there are three principal degrees of infused contemplation.[6] The first degree gives only imperfect infused union with God; the second establishes full union, but only in a temporary fashion; the third degree establishes full union permanently.

Infused recollection and the prayer of quiet comprise the first degree. In this initial stage the special infused union with God is not perfect because it is the will alone which is more directly involved. The intellect can still experience distractions.

The second degree of infused contemplation, that of full union, includes the prayer of union and the prayer of ecstasy. In this stage God possesses the powers of the soul in a manner which eliminates distractions. This union may be either ecstatic or non-ecstatic. In certain personalities the interior union with God also affects the exterior, and the use of the senses is temporarily suspended. This state is called ecstatic union. One experiences non-ecstatic union if the exterior aspect of the person is not so affected.

The third degree of infused contemplation gives full union on a permanent basis. This most special relationship with God is called the transforming union or the spiritual marriage. The mystic is habitually conscious of God's special presence. This awareness of God in the transforming union is not always of the same intensity, but it is habitual. The mystic enjoys this union both during and outside formal periods of prayer.

Connected with the tradition of infused contemplation are the terms "night of the senses" and "night of the spirit." These terms play a significant role in St. John of the Cross' description of the mystical process. What do these terms signify? The word night basically means purification or purgation. The night of the senses is the purification which accompanies the first stages of infused contemplation. The night of the spirit refers to a much deeper purification which the mystic experiences before the transforming union.

The night of the senses and the night of the spirit are particular applications of the Christian pattern of death-resurrection. The light of infused contemplation both purifies and unites. It causes death and resurrection. It purifies regarding those elements which hinder the person from a closer union with God, or, in other words, prevent a greater participation in Christ's resurrection.

The life of prayer, then, has a very close connection with the life of mysticism. Prayer, as it progresses, increasingly possesses the four characteristics of the mystical experience. The person whose prayer life grows as it should will increasingly experience God in a deeper fashion, will grow in loving wisdom of God and the things of God, will have an evolving desire to be more receptive to God and more dependent upon him, and, accompanying all this, will achieve a love union with God which results in a profound peace. It will not be a peace which rids one of all trials and difficulties. It will, however, be a peace which close union with the Lord alone can give. As St. Paul tells us, ". . . the peace of God that surpasses all understanding will guard your hearts and minds in Christ Jesus" (Phil 4:7).

Notes

1. Basil Pennington, *Challenges in Prayer* (Wilmington: Michael Glazier, Inc., 1982), p. 49.

2. John Wright, *A Theology of Christian Prayer* (New York: Pueblo, 1979), p. 101.

3. Basil Pennington, *Centering Prayer* (New York: Doubleday, 1982), p. 61.

4. *The Autobiography of St. Teresa of Avila*, translated by E. Allison Peers (New York: Doubleday, 1960), Ch. X, p. 119.

5. St. Teresa of Avila, *Interior Castle*, translated by E. Allison Peers (New York: Doubleday, 1961), Fourth Mansions, Ch. II, p. 83.

6. Joseph de Guibert, *The Theology of the Spiritual Life* (New York: Sheed and Ward, 1953), p. 332.

Chapter Five

Mysticism and Self-Identity

Our contemporary age has manifested a very significant interest in popular psychological writings. Much of this writing strives to describe the process of achieving self-identity and fulfillment. Whatever the particular psychological theory may be, it seems to have an eagerly awaiting audience. All this manifests a deeply imbedded desire within the human heart for healing, for personality growth, for achieving that mental and emotional state in which a sense of well-being is the rule rather than the exception.

Certain psychological teachings can be helpful; others, either more blatantly or more subtly, are hostile to religious principles. Paul Vitz, a psychologist himself, cogently demonstrates this in his thought-provoking book, *Psychology As Religion: The Cult Of Self-Worship.*[1]

Finding psychological teachings which are sympathetic to the Christian message is, then, not the easiest task. This no doubt explains why, among other reasons, Carl Jung has become so popular among current religious psychologists. Indeed, Jung was well aware of religion's role in personality development. One Jungian commentator says, "Some of Jung's unorthodox statements about religion have roused the hostile criticisms of thelogians, but there can be no question as to the importance Jung ascribed to the experience of God. He believed that many of the ills of the modern world were due to its being cut off from its religious roots."[2]

To be useful to the Christian, psychological teaching must blend harmoniously with the message of Jesus. Jesus is the great psychologist, the one who has the secret to the only fully authentic personality theory. Jesus knows what is good for us, what will bring us to personality maturity, what will lead to the wholeness each of us desires. Jesus is the one who can put us more and more in touch with our true selves—thus allowing us to achieve greater self-identity with the consequent sense of personal peace, fulfillment, and happiness.

Much in contemporary society goes against the teaching of Jesus. If Jesus teaches us about the true, authentic self, there are numerous cultural factors which cater to the false self, the non-authentic self. A pyschiatrist observes, "Our society is a glory-seeking, pride-oriented, dynamic system, which influences each family to influence each newborn child to predicate his or her self-acceptance on where he or she lands in the self-glorification hierarchy. Simply put, this means that we accept ourselves almost exclusively in terms of achievement and 'success', as it is measured by money, prestige, power, sexual attractiveness, or youth."[3]

The authentic self, consequently, is at odds with numerous factors in today's culture. This authentic self is the true self, the Christic self, the self made in God's image. It is the self which desires to live according to God's plan, according to his will.

The non-authentic self, on the other hand, is the self which does not want to live according to God's will. There are numerous ways in which the false self strives to inject itself. All are characterized in various degrees by a straying from the teaching and example of Christ.

The true, authentic self is not afraid to look at the false self. This is painful, but the authentic self realizes one must confront the false self in order to take the proper means to diminish its influence. The non-authentic self, on the contrary, strives to avoid consciousness of the true self so that it may, unimpeded, follow its wayward journey. If one, consequently, has little thought concerning God and the things of God, this is a good indication that the false self is exerting considerable influence over one's thoughts and activities.

Since the only real identity we have is our relationship with God in Christ—we are in God's image as mediated by Christ—we grow in achieving true self-identity through growth in the awareness that we are a unique reflection of God, that we live by his life—indeed, we participate in his life through grace. In this age of great interest in psychology, it is interesting to note that Carl Jung also links self-identity with the realization of one's God-image: "Too few people have experienced the divine image as the innermost possession of their own souls. Christ only meets them from without, never from within the soul; that is why dark paganism still reigns there."[4]

Prayer and mysticism play a profound role in achieving self-identity. In the loving quiet of prayer God reveals both himself to us and us to ourselves. These aspects are intimately connected. As God communicates knowledge concerning his loveable being, he also gives insight into ourselves, we who are in his image. As prayer grows and becomes more mystical, this insight concerning God and ourselves deepens. We become more aware of what is involved in living by the life of God, in living according to the divine image, in living a Christic existence. All these expressions point to the same reality—that we are finite expressions of the infinite, and that growth in self-identity means an increased lived-awareness of this sublime truth.

When this awareness reaches a certain consistency, we have arrived at a change in consciousness. This stage of the spiritual journey is of the utmost importance. If one goes forward after this change in consciousness, one's life will never again be the same. One has achieved a new way of comprehending the answer to the mystery of human existence.

Before this change in consciousness occurs, even the committed Christian can ask at times, as life fails to give a sufficient sense of fulfillment, "Is this all there is to life?"

This question can nag at the human heart even as one enjoys significant accomplishments, experiences the joy of the human condition, and feels a sense of love and security emanating from intimate personal relationships. "Is this all there is to life?" is a question which haunts the human heart the world over. For example, Houston Smith points to this critical issue in his discussion of Hinduism: "There comes a time," writes Aldous Huxley, "when one asks even of Shakespeare, even of Beethoven, 'is this all?'." Applying this basic question of the human heart to the context of Hinduism, Smith continues, "This is the moment Hinduism has been waiting for. As long as a person is content with the prospects of pleasure, success, or dutiful living, the Hindu sage will not be likely to disturb him beyond offering some suggestions as to how to proceed toward these goals more effectively. The critical point in life comes when these things lose their original charm and one finds oneself wishing that life had something more to offer."[5]

"Is this all there is to life?" For the Christian also, this question and the manner in which he or she confronts it, is of critical importance. It is not as though the Christian who faces this existential challenge has not previously possessed the key to life's mystery. The vision of Christian faith has already provided this key. The vision of faith, however, operates on different levels. The mature mystic, possessing a deeply operative faith, has a better grasp on how to live the mystery of life than does the non-mystic. The mystic professes the same Christian creed as does the non-mystic, but the depth of her or his faith-vision and love-dynamism allows her or him to live at a more profound level, and, consequently, at an existential depth which yields a special sense of peace and fulfillment in the Lord.

Confronting properly, then, the haunting question, "Is this all there is to life?," will lead to this deeper Christian exis- tence which will manifest that, yes, indeed, there is more to life than one had previously known. If one follows the lead of grace, and consistently lives on the level where the Christic self is dynamically operative, one will never again be haunted by the feeling that life is not yielding a sufficient sense of fulfillment.

As indicated above, living at this required depth involves a change in consciousness—it involves a change in a person's perspective. More and more one's awareness becomes God-centered, becomes Christ-centered. The awareness of the "I" is still there, but it becomes increasingly wedded to God-consciousness, to Christ-consciousness. The person progressively realizes that one possesses a Trinitarian, Christic image—a God-life—and that the only way one becomes more oneself, that is, grows in achieving self-identity, is to allow God to deepen this Trinitarian, Christic imprint. The deepening of this image, in turn, deepens one's consciousness of God.

The four mystical characteristics—having more than ordinary experience of God, being increasingly receptive to God's presence and growing in dependence on him, being a recipient of mystical knowledge, and possessing a very intimate union with God—are very much at work in this change of consciousness. The Christian realizes that consistently living these characteristics will forever dispel that haunting question, "Is this all there is to life?" Why is this? Because to live the mystical characteristics consistently is to live the God-life, the Christ-life, at such a level that one possesses the lived-answer to the above question. One experientially knows that if a person lives at a sufficient depth in Christ, it is impossible to ask, "Is this all there is to life?" One has experienced a sense of fulfillment previously unknown at the lower levels of the spiritual life. One is amazed at what happens when a person allows God to possess one as he wishes. This is not to say that one is perfectly happy, that trials and tribulations cease. Such a state is eternal life itself, the beatific vision.

Undergoing change of consciousness includes a deepened realization that one's existence is a reflection of the divine. One realizes that as Christ in his humanity reflected God in a supreme fashion, our humanities, in a lesser but still very significant manner, are also created expressions or images of God himself. We are finite reflections of the Infinite. We, indeed, help continue the Incarnation. We are extensions of Christ—an awesome privilege and responsibility.

There is, then, the most intimate connection between God's self-communication to the humanity of Christ in the hypostatic union and his self-communication to us. Rahner says, "Grace in all of us and hypostatic union in the one Jesus Christ can only be understood together, and as a unity they signify the one free decision of God for a supernatural order of salvation, for his self-communication. In Christ the self-communication of God takes place basically to all men. This is meant not in the sense that they would also have the hypostatic union as such, but rather that the hypostatic union takes place insofar as God wishes to communicate himself to all men in grace and glory."[6]

This is our glory, consequently, that God loves us and has communicated himself to us, imprinting upon us his own divine image. Growth in self-identity is growth in the realization of this magnificent truth. Growth in self-identity is growth in the realization that I must increasingly hand myself over to Christ.

Change in consciousness, therefore, means living on a deeper level. It means an increased awareness of God in Christ. It means experiencing a sense of distaste when the self is thought of apart from God. This distaste is caused by the evolving awareness that the true self, united to God, lives by his life. The self conceived of apart from God becomes, therefore, increasingly meaningless and repugnant to the person who has attained this degree of spiritual development.

Because God becomes more and more important to the person at this stage, activity takes on a different meaning and perspective. Previously, one's activity, even though performed for love of God, was more superficial. The person experienced God to a certain extent in daily activity, but his presence was often only faintly recognized. Having advanced to that deeper level of living which accompanies change of consciousness, however, the Christian now operates with a more penetrating vision. The person is much more aware of God's presence during one's activities, much more aware that one is performing these activities with God and through participation in his life. The person increasingly desires to allow Christ to be expressed through what one does. The person at this stage of the spiritual journey has achieved greater spiritual freedom regarding various works and activities. With increased awareness one realizes that the only thing that matters is that one does God's will. If this is accomplished, then the person equally experiences God and reflects his life regardless of the various circumstances involved—whether a particular activity is pleasant to perform or is done with considerable repugnance, whether it enjoys outward success and affirmation from others, or whether it is seen by others as insignificant with a consequent lack of recognition.

This new-found perspective regarding activity does not mean less devotion to what one does. Increased spiritual freedom or detachment regarding various works and activities does not mean less enthusiasm relative to the same. On the contrary, living at the deeper level or center where the true self has its source produces a greater devotion and commitment regarding whatever one does. Whether one enjoys the companionship of a friend as the two walk the seashore admiring the golden-red sunset, or whether one comforts the parents who have just lost a child in sudden and unexpected death, or whether one copes with the multiple and complex problems of inner-city ministry—whatever one does is accompanied by a deeper commitment. This more profound commitment includes the deepened realization that each activity, each experience, is a precious opportunity to love God and others. The person now more maturely realizes that to live the God-life, to witness to Christ, means to strive to give one's best in all a person does. The Christian who lives at or from the center of one's being is more fully alive than the person who lives on a more superficial level. More in touch with the true self, having a firmer grasp on one's true self-identity, the person has a devotion to duty which possesses a distinctive vitality.

As the process of change of consciousness continues with its increased grasp of self-identity, there is a corresponding process of self-integration. The more we allow God to possess us, the more we experience growth towards wholeness, towards self-integration. It is interesting to note here that in Jung's psychology, the final stage of his personality theory—called the process of individuation—also involves this key idea of self-integration. In this process Jung's archetype of the self is the catalyst: "The self . . . can include both the conscious and the unconscious. It appears to act as something like a magnet to the disparate elements of the personality and the processes of the unconscious, and is the center of this totality . . . ."[7]

The process towards greater self-identity with its accompanying process of self-integration is not without pain. Here we realize once again that the Christic pattern of death-resurrection lies at the heart of Christian existence. To achieve greater self-identity and integration involves pain. There is, for instance, the pain of allowing God's love to possess us at a deeper level. This may sound strange—that surrendering more to God's love involves suffering. There is a part of us, however, that resists God's love, and to overcome this and increasingly to abandon ourselves to God's loving guidance includes its own kind of suffering. To look at the false, ugly self—as we must in under-going change in consciousness—is a further example of the suffering involved in achieving greater self-identity. We look at the false self for a positive purpose—in order to know what we must do to lessen the false self's influence. Doing it for a positive purpose, however, does not mean that suffering is absent. Finally, we must remember that whatever suffering we experience in growth towards greater self-identity, we do so for the purpose of achieving increased purification, which, in turn, results in more intimate union with God.

The process of attaining a more meaningful contact with the Christic self—attaining greater self-identity—is enhanced in proportion to its mystical element. In other words, the more mystical the process, the more the goal is attained. Why is this? Because as the process becomes more mystical, the greater becomes the role of God. The four characteristics of mysticism become more consistently present. The person increasingly realizes that to abandon oneself more and more to God's loving guidance is the key to achieving greater self-identity. To be increasingly possessed by God is to be increasingly the true self. This state of being produces a peace beyond the comprehension of those living on a lower level of spiritual development. Indeed, to be possessed by God in his love for us is our true glory.

Notes

1. Cf. Paul Vitz, *Psychology As Religion: The Cult of Self-Worship* (Grand Rapids: Eerdman Publishing Co., 1977), p. 10.

2. Christopher Bryant, *Jung and the Christian Way* (Minneapolis: Winston-Seabury, 1983), p. 1.

3. Theodore Rubin, *Reconciliations: Inner Peace in an Age of Anxiety* (New York: The Viking Press, 1980), p. 3.

4. Carl Jung, *Psychology and Alchemy*, par. 12, as quoted in Freida Fordham, *An Introduction to Jung's Psychology* (New York: Penguin Books, 1953), pp. 74-75.

5. Houston Smith, *The Religions of Man* (New York: Harper & Row, 1958), p. 25.

6. Karl Rahner, *Foundations of Christian Faith* (New York: Seabury Press, 1978), pp. 201-202.

7. Freida Fordham, *An Introduction to Jung's Psychology* (New York: Penguin Books, 1953). p. 62.

Chapter Six

Life in the Spirit

St. Paul tells us, "We have not received the spirit of the world but the Spirit that is from God, so that we may understand the things freely given us by God" (1 Cor 2: 12). This particular text admirably serves the discussion of mysticism. Mysticism is the lived awareness, to a highly developed degree, of what it means to live the God-life. It is a profound realization of what it means to participate in God's life through grace. The above text reminds us that the Holy Spirit has been given to us to teach us how to live this God-life, this Christ-life. The Spirit perfectly understands the life of God, and he perfectly understands our participation in that life. He is the perfect teacher who instructs us how to live and develop this life, ideally to its mystical heights.

The Holy Spirit, consequently, is with us to guide us in our life in Christ. He continually desires to deepen the Christic, Trinitarian image within us. While by no means pretending to be exhaustive, let us consider some of the truths and practices pertinent to life in the Spirit.

The Spirit desires that we constantly seek out Jesus. Whatever the Spirit wants to tell us, along whatever path he desires to lead us—all this in some way is contained in the mystery of Christ. To be formed in Christ under the gentle but sure touch of the Spirit means that we must be open to the spiritual lessons contained in the various mysteries or events of Christ's life. This is especially true of the two central and summary mysteries, Christ's death and resurrection. We must consistently strive to have the proper perspective concerning these two key events. Spiritual writing has not always presented such a perspective. For many years a considerable portion of spiritual writing and teaching seemed to present the cross dimension, or dying with Christ, as if it were to receive almost exclusive attention. That we should be living resurrection upon this earth, as well as looking forward to its culmination in eternal life, was often not properly emphasized. To live resurrection in the here and now means to increasingly partake of resurrection peace, joy, happiness, and fulfillment. Our incorporation into Christ's passion and death is a means to a life of resurrection here on earth as well as in eternity.

Today, we must guard against the opposite danger—incorrectly emphasizing resurrection with the consequent effect of removing the cross aspect from its proper place in Christian consciousness. We must always be aware of the words of Paul: "For Christ did not send me to baptize but to preach the gospel, and not with the wisdom of human eloquence, so that the cross of Christ might not be emptied of its meaning" (1 Cor 1:17).

The Spirit, then, desires to lead us to a consistent and balanced contact with Christ. Some of the means we should use to assure this contact are participation in liturgy, reading of Scripture, and prayer.

The mention of prayer easily leads us to another important aspect of life in the Spirit—how the Spirit guides us in making the proper decisions in the following of Christ. Among the various purposes of prayer is seeking such guidance from the Spirit. In prayer the Christian asks for the necessary light to make decisions according to the teaching and example of Jesus. In prayer one asks for the grace to see persons, places, things, circumstances, according to a Christian perspective. Prayer, then, is necessary for proper decision-making because it is a special source of light for the intellect. Prayer is also a special source of strength for the will. Prayer gives us the strength and courage to make correct decisions even though these at times are very difficult or unpopular ones, ones which may make life unusually demanding for a period of time.

As we seek the light of the Spirit during prayer, we must be aware that not everything we originally think is an illumination of the Spirit actually is such. In other words, there are false lights or illuminations. We must, therefore, be able to distinguish between true and false lights. As St. Ignatius of Loyola tells us, we must consider the entire course of what we think are the enlightenments of the Spirit.[1] We must consider their beginning, middle, and end. If the entire course is good and directed to what is right, then we have assurance our lights are according to the Spirit. A false light could begin by presenting us with a good, but the end point, and possibly also the middle point, discloses the false light in its true character. Such a light would lead us to what is evil, or less good.

As we prayerfully consider the various options involved in a decision-making process, we begin to experience a sense of peace and clarity relative to one of the options. This usually seems to happen in a more gradual manner, but it also can occur rather suddenly. This experience of peace and clarity is one of the great signs pointing to the decision which the Spirit desires we make.

Just as we can be subjected to false lights, we can also experience false peace. For example, we can experience a certain peace because the decision we are about to make will relieve us of a considerable burden. The peace, however, is short-lived. We begin to feel dissatisfied with the prospective decision, ill-at-ease about actually choosing this particular action. Recognizing the briefly experienced peace as a false sign, we then continue the discernment process.

We must also realize that the experience of true peace in the decision-making process does not guarantee that all anxiety is removed. In choosing a certain option, we are indeed guided by the experience of peace, but there can also be certain fears attached to our choice. There can also be aspects of the decision not to our liking. The experience of peace, however, remains dominant, giving us reasonable assurance we have chosen correctly in the Spirit.

In striving to make decisions in the Spirit, we must also be aware of another important principle: as far as possible, we should never make decisions, especially important ones, when we are in a state of desolation. In such a state we are in danger of making decisions which are not in accordance with the Spirit. Let us consider some of the words of St. Ignatius concerning desolation: "I call desolation . . . darkness of soul, turmoil of spirit, inclination to what is low and earthly, restlessness rising from many disturbances and temptations which lead to want of faith, want of hope, want of love . . . ."[2]

As we progress in our discussion of principles and practices regarding life in the Spirit, let us now consider the concept of spiritual freedom. Growth in this freedom is one of the great signs of spiritual progress. Spiritual freedom is the ability to relate to persons, places, things, circumstances, and all else according to God's will. It means we are free enough to live in the manner God desires. Spiritual freedom means we are not wrongfully attached to this or that—an attachment which prevents us from following the lead of the Spirit.

As we are using the idea of spiritual freedom, a lack of such does not imply a person is not responsible for wrongful action. It simply means one abuses freedom, that one is here and now attached to a particular attitude or desire which leads one to go against the Spirit's lead.

St. Ignatius of Loyola and St. John of the Cross are two of the great masters regarding growth in spiritual freedom. They do not use the same type of language, but their message is basically the same—one must take whatever means are necessary to put oneself at the disposal of God. One must labor at breaking the inordinate attachments which lead one to go against God's will. One must develop the spiritual freedom necessary to decide according to the Spirit's guidance.

The more the mystical process develops, the more this spiritual freedom takes deeper root in a person. Growth in mysticism includes a growing desire to be possessed by

God, to do whatever he wants, to accomplish his will at all costs. All this describes a person who is truly free, a person who uses freedom to accomplish one's God-given destiny.

Growth in spiritual freedom is accompanied by growth in spiritual peace. Here, then, we wish to expand upon this concept of peace which we earlier discussed in connection with prayer and its decision-making process. For we should cultivate spiritual peace not only relative to discernment, but also as it pertains to all aspects of our lives.

To maintain oneself in a state of peace is extremely important for life in the Spirit. We can best listen to the Spirit and respond to his lights when in a basic peace of spirit. We may speak of three different kinds of this peace.

The first type is not of everyday occurrence. It is that feeling of peace which permeates all aspects of our being to such an extent that we can, as it were, almost taste the peace. We seem to feel it flowing through the total person. Again, this experience is not the ordinary fare.

A second type of peace is one which is our more customary companion on the spiritual journey. It is of a calmer nature, sometimes even accompanied by considerable spiritual dryness. It is that kind of peace which we experience on a rather daily basis. It is present amid the ordinary successes, troubles, joys, and anxieties of everyday existence. If it does not raise us to the ecstatic level of the first kind of peace, it is, nevertheless, a welcome companion. It enables us to go about our life in the Lord with a basic joy, enthusiasm, trust, and optimism.

The third kind of peace is, as is the case with the type first described, of a more rare occurence. It is that peace which we should strive for even though we are presently experiencing very significant—perhaps even severe—suffering of one kind or other. This mode of suffering has the capacity to disturb us mightily, to confuse us, to narrow our perspective. We must, then, make very special efforts to go deep down to the center of our being where there is that peace which even deep suffering cannot remove. When we reach this centerpoint, when we actuate this deep-rooted level of peace, we are in a position to confront the suffering as the Spirit desires. We are in a position to allow him to guide us through the suffering in a manner which promotes the pattern of death-resurrection. We rise from the experience more spiritually mature, persons capable of deeper love of God and neighbor.

As we progress to other attitudes necessary for life according to the Spirit, it is of great importance that we mention love of neighbor. A dynamic awareness and loving concern for our neighbor is an extremely important sign that we are truly alive in the Spirit. This seems so theoretically obvious to us, but in the day-in and day-out existence of even committed Christians this criterion does not always receive the attention it should. In his first epistle, St. John appeals to love of neighbor as a special sign of our walking in the Spirit: "Whoever says he is in the light, yet hates his brother, is still in the darkness. Whoever loves his brother remains in the light, and there is nothing in him to cause a fall" (1 Jn 2:9-10). Another passage: "Beloved, if God so loved us, we also must love one another. No one has ever seen God. Yet, if we love one another, God remains in us, and his love is brought to perfection in us" (1 Jn 4:11-12).

Flexibility of will is another indication we are properly listening to the Spirit. To determine rigidly to adhere to certain courses of action no matter what is contradictory to the concept of being open to the Spirit. A word of caution, however, is necessary here. This flexibility of spirit does not mean instability. There is a basic stability necessary in the following of Christ. This stability is itself a sign we are corresponding to the Spirit's guidance.[3] Flexibility of spirit does not mean departing from our basic way of life in Christ. The flexibility we are describing is rather an aspect of openness to the Spirit's guidance. This flexibility is a disposition which excludes a preconceived pattern of life in Christ which is hostile to the legitimate changes, modifications, and adaptations which one is called to make at certain junctures of the spiritual journey.

In discussing our life in the Spirit, we should say a few words concerning spiritual direction. The term itself basically gives its own definition. Spiritual guidance helps us lead our spiritual life—life according to the Spirit.

The role of spiritual guidance is rooted in the communal aspect of Christian existence. We do not go to God alone. In so many different ways, we are meant to help others achieve their destiny. In turn, we are meant to receive assistance from our brothers and sisters in the human family. Receiving spiritual guidance is one implementation of this social dimension of the Christian life.

There are numerous ways we receive guidance in our Christian existence. Receiving instruction through homilies and retreat conferences, attending seminars, workshops, and lectures on various aspects of the spiritual life, pertinent and sound advice received from a friend or marriage partner—these are some of the ways in which guidance comes our way.

There exists, consequently, this more general mode of spiritual direction. However, we can also greatly profit from the more individualized mode. According to this framework, one chooses a spiritual guide with whom one meets on a more or less regular basis. The frequency depends on various factors. Beginners in the spiritual life usually require more frequent meetings until they become solidly grounded in fundamentals. Times of particular trial offer another occasion for more frequent sessions with a guide, as do times of critical decision-making.

The fundamental task of the spiritual guide is to help one discern the action of the Spirit. To achieve this, the guide must be a good and patient listener. As one commentator says, "A lot of people expect us to question them, but it is important to accustom them not to count on our questions, but to talk on their own accord. It is only after we have listened to them for a long time like this that we shall we able to ask the essential question."[4]

Listening is of such importance because it allows the guide to see how the Spirit seems to be leading this particular person. Knowing this, the guide can, asking the proper questions and making pertinent comments, intelligently make his or her contributions in aiding the person's ongoing openness to the Spirit. The guide, consequently, is not out front, as it were, leading the person according to a preconceived path of how he or she is to follow the Spirit. Of course, there are certain fundamentals of the spiritual life which are the same for all, and a good guide will operate according to these. Since each person is unique, however, the Spirit leads each according to a pattern which will in various ways differ from that of others.

It is obvious, then, that a person should choose a guide with whom one feels comfortable and with whom one is willing to share the basic essentials of one's interior life. Unless the guide knows these, he or she cannot properly aid the person in following the lead of the Spirit.

Besides being a good listener, a guide should possess other basic qualities. One should obviously possess requisite knowledge of the spiritual life. Requisite knowledge is a relative concept. For example, the knowledge required to direct a beginner in the spiritual life is obviously less than that required to direct one who has entered the mystical state. A good guide should also possess considerable prudence—to know how and when to apply spiritual principles to particular individuals. Knowing how to point out errant ways is also of obvious importance. To possess not only a theoretical knowledge of the spiritual life, but also that knowledge gained through one's own living of the ways of the Spirit is a desired characteristic. These, then, are some of the qualities a good spiritual guide should possess.

As we near the end of our considerations regarding life in the Spirit, it is most appropriate that we make mention of Mary. Just as Mary cooperated with the Holy Spirit in bringing Jesus into this world, so is her cooperation with the Spirit present regarding each of us. Under the Spirit she desires to bring us to maturity in Christ. Her concern, her care, her love for us is beyond our full comprehension. Under her maternal protection, we go to the Father with Christ and by the Spirit. Truly she is our spiritual mother:

"Standing by the cross of Jesus were his mother and his mother's sister, Mary the wife of Clopas, and Mary of Magdala. When Jesus saw his mother and the disciple there whom he loved, he said to his mother, 'Woman, behold, your son.' Then he said to the disciple, 'Behold, your mother.'" (Jn 19: 25-27).

As we surrender more and more to the Spirit and Mary and become increasingly formed in the image of Christ, our lives become more mystical. We grow in the awareness that truly to live is to live the God-life in Christ. Increasingly we live by God's love, by his wisdom, by his strength. Our awareness, and, indeed, our entire persons become increasingly transformed in God. An aspect of this awareness is a growing realization that, "We have not received the spirit of the world but the Spirit that is from God, so that we may understand the things freely given us by God" (1 Cor 2:12).

Notes

1. Cf. *The Spiritual Exercises of St. Ignatius*, translated by L. Puhl (Westminster: Newman Press, 1951), Nos. 332-334.

2. Ibid., No. 317.

3. Cf. St. Francis de Sales, *On the Love of God*, translated by J. Ryan (New York: Doubleday, 1963), Bk VIII, Ch. 13, pp. 84-87.

4. Jean Laplace, *The Direction of Conscience* (New York: Herder and Herder, 1967), p.173.

Chapter Seven

Mysticism and Action

We live in a highly active culture. The fast-paced existence of industrialized-technological societies leaves one almost breathless at times. We can and should, however, ask ourselves what is the real worth of all this activity? Much of it is good, prompted by worthy motivation—parents, for instance, working tirelessly for the proper rearing of their children. At the same time, a considerable portion of human activity comes forth from immoral motivation—greed, lust, hatred, envy, and the rest.

Regarding the good portion of human activity, even this often seems to lack a certain depth. When this depth is lacking, people are actually living more on the surface of reality. Even though one would basically be living a good life, a person misses much when he or she fails to live on a deeper level. To be concrete, two persons could perform what seems to be the same act of love towards one's neighbor. One of the persons, however, produces the act more from a surface-type level, while the other calls forth the act from the depths of the true self. This latter act possesses much more dynamism than the former; its qualitative worth is considerably greater.

The study of mysticism yields an unmistakable fact concerning human activity: the mystic is one whose activity is permeated with a deeply rooted dynamism, a dynamism charged with true vitality precisely because of the mystic's very close union with God, this God who is infinite act. The mystic, indeed, is very conscious of living life to the fullest.

We must be careful to understand what living life to the fullest means for the mystic. First of all, it obviously differs from the meaning attached to this phrase by those worldly individuals who seek the pleasures of this world with little or no thought of God. For the mystic, living life to its fullest also differs from that perception of the phrase which even the ordinary good person has. Such a person, while living the essentials of religion, engages in a considerable portion of his or her activity without a consistent seeking of light and strength from God. For the mystic, on the other hand, living life to its fullest means that she or he has, in a very lofty manner, handed the self over to God to be possessed by him. She or he cannot conceive of a meaningful life apart from God. For the mystic, to think of the self is to realize the only true self is the divinized self, the self united to God. It is from this depth of perception that the mystic's activity flows forth. It is this lived awareness of the Christic self that clothes the mystic's actions with such great worth.

An important aspect of the mystic's living life to the fullest is a great concentration on the present. We are past, present and future persons. The past still influences us in many ways. For example, recall of what led to past mistakes can aid us in avoiding the same in the present and future. The thought of the future is important also, as we prudently plan for its arrival, as we derive enthusiasm from the pursuit of goals not yet attained. Also, the thought of our absolute future—eternal life with God—is very important. We are, then, past and future persons. We are also present persons. Concentration on the present is extremely important. We cannot relive the past; and our future upon this earth is unpredictable in many ways, including its time-length; finally, our absolute future—eternal life—is being shaped by the way we use the present. The mystic is very aware of all this. The mystic has a special capacity to develop the growth potential of each day. The mystic has an abiding desire to try to use the present to the utmost in loving God and neighbor.

The mystic, consequently, admirably uses the present to develop his or her divinized humanity to ever higher degrees of maturity. Contrary to what many seem to think concerning the mystic, the person is more human precisely because of his or her mysticism. There is a greater sensitivity to all things human. For example, the mystic loves deeply, greatly appreciates the beauties of nature, is distressed at the evils present within the human condition, rejoices at all the manifestations of human goodness—and all this in a manner which is more advanced than would be the case if the person were not blessed with mystical union with God.

The mystic does not achieve this level of human life without an experientially learned perspective of what the mystical life means regarding one's humanity. There can be the temptation to think that the mystical life further removes one from things human and that greater divinization means, in certain ways, leaving behind what is human. The true mystic, however, overcomes this false view and realizes that mysticism does not remove one from the human condition, but allows the person to live it more perfectly. Divinization—graced union with God, a union highly developed in the mystical life—perfects that which is human, rather than making it less human. What Rahner says regarding the humanity of Christ is proportionately true of us: "Christ is therefore man in the most radical way, and his humanity is . . . the most free not in spite of, but because it has been assumed . . . ."[1] In other words, the human freedom of Christ and all other aspects of his humanity are supremely perfect because of their extremely close union with the person who is Son. The second person of the Trinity, in assuming a human nature, has raised that humanity to the fullest heights possible, this humanity which is perfectly submissive to the divine will.

To a far lesser degree, but, nevertheless, in a very real and sublime fashion, our humanities are raised to a new level of perfection precisely because of our graced union with God. The mystic, having highly developed this union, consequently lives the human in a manner which surpasses that of the less advanced.

One aspect of our personhood is its uniqueness. Applying the above principle—that the closer one's union with God, the more fulfilled are all aspects of the person—we see that we become more unique the closer we come to God.

This is contrary to what many seem to think—they feel that if they get too close to God, their individuality will be smothered. Indeed, the opposite is true. One's uniqueness becomes more developed, more attractive, more expressive of the true self, in proportion to union with God.

Attached to the concept of personal uniqueness is the idea of personal mission. John Henry Cardinal Newman tells us, "Everyone who breathes, high and low, educated and ignorant, young and old, man and woman, has a mission, has a work. We are not sent into this world for nothing; we are not born at random. . . . God sees every one of us; He creates every soul, He lodges it in a body, one by one, for a purpose."[2] Mystical union with God heightens this awareness of personal mission. The mystic, keenly conscious of her or his uniqueness, keenly conscious that she or he is a unique, finite expression of the infinite God, marvels at one's special privilege and responsibility. The mystic is keenly aware that each of us has the grand opportunity of giving one's humanity to Christ. To the extent one does so, Christ has the opportunity of continuing his life and mission in us according to the uniqueness of each one's personhood. To the extent one refuses Christ, Christ loses this opportunity.

We must not succumb to the temptation, then, which suggests that, because our lives are externally so ordinary, we have little to offer Christ and the world. Rahner has words of advice for us in this regard: "Let us take a good look at Jesus who had the courage to lead an apparently useless life for thirty years. We should ask him for the grace to give us to understand what his hidden life means for our religious existence."[3] Notice that Rahner says "apparently," for in reality Jesus' hidden life at Nazareth was supremely worthwhile because he was doing the will of his Father. No matter how simple and prosaic our lives may appear, consequently, they, too, are worthwhile to the extent we embrace God's will.

Our personal uniqueness, our personal mission, will, in general, be lived out in the midst of the ordinary. Usually, we will express our love for neighbor in commonplace ways, not in the heroic rescue of others from burning buildings. For most of us, we will not express our creativity as did Beethoven in his timeless music or as did Shakespeare in his priceless writings. We rather must strive to be creative in such ways as preparing innovative meals for others or by bringing a touch of freshness to our personal relationships. These, then, are some examples of the ordinariness which, for the most part, provides the setting for our lives.

This ordinary setting, however, refers to the external framework of our existence. If we approach this commonplace exterior with deep faith, hope and love, then the ordinary becomes truly extraordinary. Our lives become extraordinary testimonies of what a life in Christ means to the world. The lives of the mystics tell us this—if we have ears to listen! Their activity, so highly expressive of their unique selves and personal missions, possessed such great value precisely because of the depth at which they lived—because of the depth of their faith, hope and love.

In our present discussion concerning mysticism and action, it is certainly appropriate that we briefly address the idea of mysticism and involvement with social issues. Many apparently think that the mystic is a withdrawn type of person, one who is not very practical, one who is not very aware of pressing social problems. It must be admitted that a considerable portion of the traditional mystical literature has lent itself to this erroneous view of the mystic. Such literature has often discussed in an almost exclusive fashion the mystic's very direct relationship with God in mystical contemplation. The mystic's apostolic life—finding God in the service of neighbor—has often received little or no attention.

Indeed, spiritual literature in general—not just that dealing with mysticism—was for many years often guilty of the same error. The separation of personal spirituality from social action was not an uncommon occurrence in spiritual writing. In recent years there happily has been a change. Francis Meehan observes, "Here I wish to affirm that the social movement among spiritual people is not merely a fad, but a maturing consciousness of what it means to be a spiritual person."[4]

Not only do we see this current interest of linking spirituality in general with social involvement, but we also find a similar interest regarding mysticism in particular. For example, William Johnston says, "The task confronting us today is to unite activism and mysticism."[5]

We should make it perfectly clear that the true mystics of past generations did not themselves separate personal spirituality and apostolic activity, whether that activity included direct social involvement or not. The mystic sees more clearly than does the non-mystic the necessary link between apostolic interest and the rest of the spiritual life. The mystic profoundly realizes that love for Christ includes love for the world that belongs to him.

Love for the world means helping to increase its goodness while simultaneously working to lessen its evil aspect. Promoting the world's goodness, in turn, means helping to further permeate secular realities with the truths of the Gospel; for, contrary to the thinking of those given over to secularism, the world truly progresses only in proportion to its union with Christ. This union, far from hindering secular realities in achieving their goals, enhances the process. The analogy of friendship offers insight in this regard. When another assumes me in friendship, my opportunity for growth as this unique individual is not thwarted but increased. In taking me in friendship, the other in various ways helps me to grow. The situation is similar regarding Christ's assuming or uniting to himself secular realities. Such a union enhances, not hinders, their opportunity to fulfill their God-given purposes.[6] For example, the more the economic order is influenced by the spirit of the Gospel, the more it attains its purpose of providing for the basic needs of all.

If the mystic clearly sees the connection between loving Christ and neighbor and being concerned with the secular, he or she also realizes proper precautions must accompany those who are called into the marketplace. One's horizontal relationship with God—finding him in the service of others within the human condition—must be balanced with a healthy vertical relationship with God—meeting him more directly through such practices as prayer. The proper balance between action and contemplation has perennially offered a challenge to spirituality. Theoretically we see what the balance should be, but attaining this in the practical order is not the easiest accomplishment. While some neglect the horizontal dimension, most seem to have to guard against over-involvement in horizontal activity. They, indeed, must guard against succumbing, in various degrees, to an extreme horizontalism. Rahner describes this as follows: "What we are referring to here is a radical horizontalism. In other words that doctrine and that interpretation of life which regards the task of the Church properly speaking consisting in one thing alone: a responsibility for mankind, for the human society. 'God' is reduced to a mere cipher (old-fashioned and replaceable or for various reasons not indispensable)."[7]

We have been considering some ideas concerning mysticism and action. The overriding idea has been that growth in mysticism does not make one less apt for authentic activity, but more so. The mystic is more effective, more productive in his or her activity than is the non-mystic. The theological fact behind this is a simple one: the mystic, very closely united to God, is more capable of authentic activity than is the non-mystic precisely because he or she shares more in God's own power of activity. To be closer to God is truly to be more active in the authentic meaning of the phrase.

Notes

1. Karl Rahner, *Foundations of Christian Faith* (New York: Seabury Press, 1978), p. 226.

2. John Henry Cardinal Newman, *Discourses Addressed to Mixed Congregations* (London: Longmans, Green and Co., 1906), pp. 111-112.

3. Karl Rahner, *Spiritual Exercises* (New York: Sheed and Ward, 1964), p.160.

4. Francis Meehan, *A Contemporary Social Spirituality* (New York: Orbis Books, 1982), p. 2.

5. William Johnston, *Christian Mysticism Today* (Harper & Row: San Francisco, 1984), p. 152.

6. Johannes Metz, "The Christian and the World," in *The Sacred and the Secular*, edited by Michael Taylor (Engelwood Cliffs: Prentice-Hall, 1968) p. 78.

7. Karl Rahner, *Theological Investigations*, Vol. XIV (New York: Seabury Press, 1976), p. 296.

Chapter Eight

Mysticism and Community

One of the false views regarding mysticism sees the mystic as not very concerned about the communal aspect of Christianity. This erroneous view considers the mystic as greatly interested in vertical relationship with God but rather unconcerned with horizontal relationship, which includes, of course, interaction with others. All this is far from the truth. We saw in our previous chapter that all aspects of the human person are brought to fulfillment proportionate to one's union with God. The more closely one is united to God, consequently, the more developed becomes that person's communal dimension or sense of community.

All the various dimensions of a person develop together as he or she travels the spiritual journey toward closer union with God. There is, then, no conflict between one aspect of a person and another. For example, one's uniqueness and one's thrust toward community, toward union with others, are not in conflict, but rather mutually influence each other. They exist harmoniously together. Rahner observes,

> But if today we are moving more and more towards the unity of a single history of the world and towards the development of the human community into a closer social network, and if we see that a person cannot discover his personhood and uniqueness by looking for them as something absolutely contrary to his social nature, but can only discover them within

his social nature and in function of this social nature; and if there is a relationship of mutual conditioning between love of God and love of neighbor, and hence if love for one's neighbor is not merely a secondary moral consequence of a proper relationship with God; and if, beyond this, love of neighbor cannot merely mean a private relationship to another individual, but also means something social and political, and implies responsibility for social and political structures within which love for one's neighbor can or cannot be practiced, then it also follows from all this that basically it would be a late bourgeois conception to think that religion has nothing essential to do with society and with church. We are aware today in a quite new and inescapable way that man is a social being, a being who can exist only within inter-communication with others throughout all of the dimensions of human existence.[1]

The mystic, possessing a deepened insight concerning God and his creation, is especially aware that God has created us social beings and that this fundamental truth has continual application along the spiritual journey. Growth in mystical insight gives increased awareness concerning the complementarity between one's individuality and one's thrust towards union with others. The more a person's uniqueness or individuality develops, the more one has to contribute to community; conversely, the more one properly interacts with others, the more that person develops as a unique individual.

The communal aspect of the Christian life comes into play in a variety of ways—including membership in the Church, marriage and family, membership in religious orders and congregations, membership in groups promoting peace and justice. This, of course, is not an exhaustive listing; nor do we intend to give an exhaustive commentary concerning mysticism and the implementation of the communal aspect of Christianity. Rather, we will limit ourselves to a few remarks.

The mystic has a profound respect for the efficacy of group or communal effort. For example, it is no accident that many of the Church's communal movements have been founded by mystics. These men and women had a deep insight into the value of communal apostolic effort precisely because of their mysticism, not in spite of it. Concerning the mystic's membership in that community which is the universal Church, we will make some comments a bit later.

Regarding the mystic's relationship with others in general, we must consider a twofold aspect. One looks to the mystic's awareness of need for others; the other aspect concerns the mystic's healthy independence regarding others. Let us take a brief look at these two facets which at first may seem to be at odds with each other but actually are not.

Growth in the mystical life produces an increased awareness that one is in the image of God. This maturing awareness regarding one's own true identity concomitantly gives an increased awareness concerning the divine image in others. This provides a fundamental, solid basis for proper relationship with others. This awareness not only helps us to relate properly to others, but reproduces in us a desire to interact with them.

Growth in the mystical life also produces a gradual purgation which includes an increasing control over wrongful pride. This is especially true in the so-called passive purgation of the spirit, during which God's special purifying grace reaches into the person's more hidden recesses where pride is more resistant to the more ordinary efforts aimed at its curbing. In turn, this curbing of pride makes the mystic much more suitable for interaction with others. How many of the problems between individuals emanate from the wrongful pride of one or both?

The mystical process, then, produces an increased awareness of the divine image and a lessening of pride's capacity to set up barriers which hinder proper interaction with others. Both of these make the mystic better able to implement the communal aspect of one's Christian personality.

So also does the sense of helplessness which the mystical process produces. The more one progresses along the mystical path, the more the person realizes one's helplessness without God. Mysticism, consequently, produces a desire to abandon oneself increasingly to the ever-loving and all-powerful God. The more the mystic does this, the stronger she or he becomes: "I will rather boast most gladly of my weaknesses, in order that the power of Christ may dwell with me. Therefore, I am content with weaknesses . . . for the sake of Christ; for when I am weak, then I am strong" (2 Cor 12:9-10).

This sense of helplessness not only thrusts the mystic into greater union with God; it also makes the mystic more conscious of the need for others. Concomitant with the mystic's growing abandonment to God is a maturing insight that this abandonment includes a striving to live more according to God's designs. One extremely important aspect of God's plan for us is to be properly dependent upon our fellow human beings. In so many ways God intends that we come to him through the help of others, just as he intends that we in turn are kindly and helpful companions to our brothers and sisters along the spiritual journey.

If the mystical process helps one to be properly dependent upon others, it also aids the mystic in becoming properly independent. This is a grand and beautiful disposition to behold in another—to see a person who realizes the need for others, but also to observe that person as not being morbidly and slavishly dependent. How many problems arise in relationships because a person is overly dependent on others? The mystic has learned to achieve the proper and relatively delicate balance between dependence and independence. Mysticism vividly reveals our need for others, but also prevents a slavish dependence. Firmly united to the all-powerful God, the mystic, while clearly recognizing one's need for other human beings, does not overestimate this fact. For the mystic, God clearly is the absolutely unshakable foundation of one's existence, the only absolutely necessary one.

As we proceed to consideration of membership in the Church—a very obvious implementation of the Christian's communal dimension—we can profit by listening to the words of Rahner: "An absolutely individual Christianity in the most personal experience of grace and ecclesial Christianity are no more radically opposed than are body and soul, than are man's transcendental essence and his historical constitution, or than are individuality and intercommunication. The two condition each other mutually. The very thing we are from God is mediated in concreteness of history by what we call church. And it is only in and through this mediation that it becomes our own reality and our salvation in full measure. For this reason church exists and has to exist."[2] Simply put, the Christian is called to life within the Church.

The Christian mystic realizes this. Not all mystics have avoided painful moments of tension within the institutional Church; but the authentic mystic does not cut ties with the Church no matter how great such problems may seem. The mystic, so closely united with Jesus, will not separate himself or herself from this Church of which Christ is the head. The mystic sees that union with Christ and union with the Church are most intimately connected. Authentic mysticism has its roots deeply imbedded in the life of the Church. William Johnston observes, "It is precisely by hearing the word and participating in the sacraments, particularly the Eucharist, that I am drawn into the mystery of Christ and into the mystical life. Moreover, word and sacrament form liturgy and community. Mysticism has a strong communal dimension."[3]

There is, then, the greatest harmony between authentic mysticism and Church. It is true that the Church has traditionally taken a certain cautious approach towards mysticism. This is so because there is a necessity to distinguish true from false mysticism.

There have indeed been sufficient instances of false mysti- cism to justify this caution. There was, for example, the false mysticism of Michael Molinos in the 17th century. Included in his false teaching was an incorrect notion of mystical passivity. This error included the idea that it is not necessary to make efforts to resist temptation. This, taught Molinos, would be a violation of passivity before God. In fact, mystical passivity does not excuse one from action. As we stated earlier, it increases a person's true activity. Mystical passivity or receptivity means that the person is very much open to God's guidance, is very much aware of being dependent upon God, is keenly conscious of striving to do God's will in all things—including taking the proper measures to resist temptation. Mystical passivity, therefore, increases one's union with God, and, consequently, brings about activity which is more God-directed, and hence more dynamic and of higher quality.

Other errors involving erroneous mysticism include mistaking hallucinations or the effects of a wild and uncontrolled imagination to be mystical revelations. A further example of an unhealthy mysticism is placing too much emphasis on the non-essential elements of mystical experience. For example, some mystics experience visions and elevations of the body, as well as other extraordinary, but non-essential mystical phenomena. Since these do not constitute essential mysticism, a person can be a mystic without experiencing such phenomena. To over-emphasize the importance of these extraordinary but non-essential mystical elements would, therefore, be erroneous.

It is necessary, consequently, that the Church take proper precautions to distinguish true from erroneous mysticism. Regarding authentic mysticism, it is completely compatible with the life of the Church. As a matter of fact—as we have already seen—developed mysticism, whether in its classical or more ordinary form, is nothing else than the full flowering of the Christian life itself. Obviously, then, mysticism pre-eminently belongs to the life of the Church. Contrary to what some apparently think, what the Church needs is more, not fewer, mystics.

Notes

1. Karl Rahner, *Foundations of Christian Faith* (New York: The Seabury Press, 1978), p. 323.

2. Ibid., p. 389.

3. William Johnston, *Christian Mysticism Today* (San Francisco: Harper & Row, 1984), p. 18.

Chapter Nine

The Mysticism of Everyday

There is a movement today which is striving to make mysticism more accessible to committed Christians. This movement is directing attention to the mystical core and seed which is in every Christian, although in many cases this core apparently does not develop into what is more strictly understood as mysticism. Even regarding this more strict use of the word mysticism, however, there is a growing realization that true mysticism can exist even though one does not experience classical mysticism, or, as it has been traditionally called, infused contemplation. There is, then, a current interest in that mysticism which has a variety of names: latent mysticism, ordinary mysticism, the mysticism of everyday life. Harvey Egan observes, "Those authors, therefore, who explicate mysticism as a way of life, a way of existing, as a fundamental openness to the mystery of life, a way which may or may not be punctuated by extraordinary experiences, seem to be on the right track. To be sure, some of these authors too easily equate mysticism with religious experience or spiritual life in general. Still, there is a sense in which mysticism is radical religious experience, the very core of the spiritual life, and the heart of authentic human living in both its individual and social aspects."[1]

In this our final chapter, consequently, we will concentrate our efforts on what may be called the mysticism of everyday. We are not addressing this issue for the first time. The concept, if not the name, has been present in many of our previous discussions. This last chapter, however, will allow us to address the idea of the mysticism of everyday in a more succinct and summary fashion.

As we begin our discussion, it will be helpful to repeat some of the things we said earlier concerning the basic meaning of the word mysticism and its application to Christianity. The term mysticism is related to the word mystery. Mystery, in turn, suggests that which is hidden or secret. In applying the term to Christianity we have what is called the mystery of Christ. God, the ultimate mystery, the ultimate hidden one, reveals himself and his plan for us through his Son, Jesus Christ. We are initiated into this mystery of Christ at baptism. Through Christian faith we achieve a knowledge of God and the things of God which is beyond those who do not possess this gift of faith. The hiddenness of God becomes, in certain ways, revealed to us. God, though, still remains mystery, for even with faith we do not fully understand him. Even with faith, we possess only a finite knowing—we cannot, consequently, perfectly comprehend the infinite God.

Through our assimilation to Christ, however, we do grasp much about God and the plan he has designed for us in Jesus. Through our incorporation into Christ, consequently, we truly are mystics in the very basic sense—we are ones who have been initiated into the mystery of Christ. Generally, however, the words mysticism and mystic are applied only to those who have developed their life in Christ— their participation in the mystery of Christ—to a high degree.

We must assume a balanced position regarding this fundamental stage of mysticism. On the one hand, we must realize the word mystic is usually not applied relative to this first level. On the other hand, we cannot completely dismiss this most general application of the word mystic. Through baptism in Christ we participate in God's own life, and this participation is the basis for the mystical life taken in the strictest sense; for when this God-life matures to a high degree, one enters the mystical state. The previously quoted words of Thils are, then, again appropriate for our present discussion: "Every Christian will understand. . . .

that this participation in divine life is, of its vary nature, the mystical life in germ. . . ."[2]

Giving proper attention to the very first and fundamental level of mysticism is important, consequently, because it reminds us that mysticism in the strictest sense is the relatively full development of that life Christians receive in baptism. Giving proper attention to this first level of mysticism—Christian mysticism taken in its broadest sense—is also important because it gives us occasion to remark that one must usually live on this level for a considerable time before arriving at the mystical state. It is true that God in extraordinary fashion can quickly raise one to the heights of mysticism. His usual pattern, however, is a more gradual leading of a person through the mystical process. As we conclude our remarks regarding the first stage of mysticism, it is obvious that the concept of the mysticism of everyday aptly applies here; for every day we are called to live the mystery of Christ.

The idea of mystical process referred to above easily leads us to the next level of mysticism. On this level, a person participates in the mystical life strictly-so-called, but only sporadically. In other words, the person experiences mystical acts, but these are not present consistently, a condition which would situate the person in the mystical state. These mystical acts partake of the four characteristics of mysticism. We have mentioned these on numerous occasions; there is, consequently, no need to repeat them here in full measure. It suffices to say that a mystical act gives a more than ordinary experience of God, a more than ordinary sense of being possessed and guided by him, a more than ordinary sense of being dependent upon him. An example of a mystical act is the special experience, on a particular occasion, of God's love, a special experience of being drawn into this love, of being guided by it, of being dependent upon it.

A person who experiences mystical acts on an occasional basis participates, at these times, in the mystical life in the stricter meaning of the term. This is so because the characteristics of strict mysticism are present, if only briefly.

Here, again, though, such a person is usually not called a mystic—a term traditionally reserved for those who experience mystical acts consistently.

It is evident how one experiencing these rather isolated, but very real, mystical acts is participating in the mysticism of everyday. People in great numbers, it seems, do not enter the mystical state, but it does seem that many receive these mystical acts or experiences on an occasional basis. These acts are woven into the fabric of everyday existence. While no one individual who is not in the mystical state will experience such acts on a consistent basis, still the number who do experience them on any one day is conceivably a very large number. In other words, the mysticism of every day, relative to this second level of Christian mysticism, is very much alive when we consider the total Christian community.

For some, the experience of sporadic mystical acts will gradually become more frequent. Eventually these acts achieve that consistent frequency which places a person in the mystical state. This state we equate with the third and final of the traditional three stages of the spiritual life. The reader will recall these stages: the purgative stage or the way of beginners; the illuminative stage or the way of proficients; the unitive stage or the way of the perfect.

The unitive stage, then, is the earthly goal of the spiritual pilgrim. We must remind ourselves, however, that attainment of the unitive stage does not mean that further development is impossible. Growth is always possible— there are various degrees of spiritual maturity in the unitive state. One can always grow in faith, hope and love. We should say, therefore, that the unitive stage marks the arrival of relatively full or perfect spiritual development. The words full and perfect denote that a person has achieved a very high degree of spiritual maturity, while the word relatively very importantly points out that further growth is still possible.

Do many enter this unitive stage of spiritual development? We can offer only educated guesses. We cannot judge the inner holiness of individuals as does God. We should, however, avoid two extremes in the matter. One extreme view suggests that unitive holiness is of rare occurence, and only a select few attain it. The other view suggests that practically all who enter upon the spiritual journey eventually attain the unitive stage. The truth seems to lie between these two extreme views. On the one hand, and contrary to what some spiritual writers seem to indicate, a quite significant number of committed Christians do seem to enter the unitive stage. On the other hand, it is unlikely that the vast majority of those entering upon a serious spiritual life attain unitive holiness. The path to the unitive stage is a demanding one, and it does not seem that all who enter upon the spiritual journey are willing to submit to what is involved in attaining the unitive degree of spiritual development.

The person who has achieved unitive holiness has achieved a very close, loving union with God. The person experiences God on a level unknown to those still walking in the lower realms of the spiritual journey. Because of the person's very intimate union with God, he or she has attained experiential knowledge of God and the things of God which the less advanced do not possess. The person has a very keen sense of dependence upon God, a very keen awareness of what it means to be guided by the Spirit, a highly developed consciousness of what it means to live the God-life, the Christ-life. In other words, the person lives the characteristics of mysticism in a highly developed manner.

One in the unitive stage, then, has achieved the mystical state. In this state one lives the mystical characteristics either according to the classical categories or in a more ordinary fashion. One who lives classical mysticism experiences God in a most special fashion. Through the words of St. Teresa of Avila we have described this very special sense of God's presence in chapter four.

Given the theme of our present chapter, the mysticism of everyday, here and now we wish to concentrate on the more ordinary mode of existence in the unitive or mystical state.

We simply call this way ordinary mysticism. The one living ordinary mysticism in the unitive state will experience the characteristics of mysticism in a consistent fashion as does the classical mystic, but in a more subdued manner. So subdued may be the person's experience that, as a result, he or she may not recognize oneself as a mystic. This explains why such mysticism is also called latent or hidden mysticism.

Currently there seems to be a growing conviction that these ordinary mystics are greater in number than previously thought. These mystics live unitive holiness, but, unlike classical mystics, they do not experience the special graces of infused contemplation which give a most special awareness of close union with God. The ordinary mystic, nevertheless, lives on a profoundly deep level. He or she is in most intimate contact with the Christic self, and this self is very dynamically and consistently expressed in love for God and neighbor. The person, on a daily basis, profoundly lives the mystery of Christ. His or her mysticism is consistently expressed amidst the myriad events of life within the human condition—that condition which includes laughter and tears, success and failure, companionship and loneliness, action and repose, pain and joy. If those living on the first two levels of mysticism manifest elements of the mysticism of everyday, those on the third level—those in the mystical state—do so in a pre-eminent fashion. Again, there are both classical and ordinary mystics living in this unitive stage, and while one can correctly use the phrase, the mysticism of everyday, in reference to classical mystics, we think it is a most appropriate term to use in reference to those who are ordinary or latent mystics.

For years many committed Christians have looked upon mysticism as strange, extremely esoteric, and not a subject which should be of particular interest to themselves. The concept of the mysticism of everyday has the potential to dispel such ideas, for it emphasizes the fact that all have the seeds of mysticism through the life of baptism itself, and that the mystical state—in either its ordinary or classical forms—is the earthly culmination of this life. Simply put, mysticism in its full development is the Christian life itself in its full development. Mysticism is living the mystery of Christ to the fullest. Mysticism is transformation in Christ.

Notes

1. Harvey Egan, *What Are They Saying About Mysticism?* (New York: Paulist Press, 1982), pp. 117-118.

2. Gustave Thils, *Christian Holiness* (Tielt, Belgium: Lannoo, 1963), p. 557.